GOD
Is Faithful
Stories That Inspire

Authors for Christ

Editing /Interior Book Design / Layout
CBM Christian Book Editing

www.christian-book-editing.com
Cover Design: CBM

Dedication

We overcome by the blood of the Lamb
and by the word of our testimony.
(Rev. 12:11)

First and foremost, we dedicate this book to the Lord Jesus Christ, who is the Rock of Our Salvation. Thank you, Jesus, for the price that you paid. Thank you for your death, burial and resurrection. Thank you for the Cross, Lord Jesus.

Secondly, this book is dedicated to you. May you find grace, encouragement, hope and abundant blessings as you read the wonderful teachings, testimonies and stories within.

No matter what you may be going through, or what you are contending for, remember, in Christ, you are loved with an everlasting love, highly-favored and precious in the sight of God.

We would also like to thank each of the authors who have participated in this book. Your testimonies are a blessing to read and share the love and redeeming passion that is available to all through Christ. As we have been blessed in reading your writings, we know that others will be also.

Table of Contents

CONTENTS

GOD USES ORDINARY PEOPLE TO DO EXTRAORDINARY THINGS

Barry D. Voss

"Brothers think of what you were when you were called. Not many of you were wise by human standards; not many were influential; not many were of noble birth. But God chose the foolish things of the world to shame the wise; God chose the weak things of the world to shame the strong. He chose the lowly things of this world and the despised things--and the things that are not--to nullify the things that are, so that no one may boast before him." (1 Corinthians 1:26-29)

As a Christian, one thing that intrigues me is how Jesus chose 12 ordinary people to be his first disciples. These men had limited skills, obscure occupations and no public platform. Why would Jesus pick such ordinary and insignificant people to build the foundation of His church on earth? It makes no earthly sense! But as we now know from Scripture, Jesus did many things that make no sense to man but make perfect sense in God's kingdom. Through 11 of these men, the number of followers of Jesus now totals more than 2.2 billion people on the earth!! That's more than any other faith and roughly one third of the world's population.

Since the beginning of the Church it is through such ordinary men and women that God has produced this extraordinary growth of His kingdom here on earth. People like Martin Luther, Dwight Moody, Florence Nightingale, Adoniram Judson, Mother Theresa, Bill Bright, Loren Cunningham, Rosa Parks, Rick Warren and Billy Graham come to my mind. None of these people were well known before God called them into ministry for Him. Yet each has had a profound impact on the world and the Christian faith.

I, too, am an ordinary person. You've probably never even heard of me (and likely won't). And yet God has called me into ministry for him as well, just like so many others before me and those who have yet to be called. So, who am I? Well, let me tell you a little bit about my story.

I grew up in a Christian home and have known Jesus all my life. But knowing Jesus and following Him are two different things. For most of my life I attended church and served in the church, but I wasn't really living my life for Him. Sadly, I see this in many Christians I know or have met as well. But I understand it because I've been there. It is easy to get caught up in the pursuit of a career, a family, or other personal interests, and to keep our faith inside the church on Sundays instead of in our words and deeds every day.

So, what was it that caused me to take my faith more seriously? Well, I believe it's the same cause for everyone

- the Holy Spirit! God found a way to get my attention and show me that I was living for myself and not Him!

In 1996 He led me to sign up for a mission trip to the nation of Kazakhstan (our pastor was part of the teaching team). I felt God's call to go but had no idea what I would do as part of the team. The Mission Team Leader asked me to bring my guitar and lead worship for the American team that was going, and I was glad to have a role on the trip. God also had me participate in the conference with the local worship team, few of whom spoke English, where I could use the musical gifts that He had given to me. But God had even bigger plans.

During one day of the conference one of the attending pastors from Uzbekistan shared a testimony that spoke to my heart. He had been in prison for Christ and beaten for his faith. But I suddenly realized that I had suffered nothing for my faith. In that moment, the Holy Spirit convicted me of my lack of true faith and trust in God and revealed to me that I needed to live my entire life for Him. So, I came back from Kazkhstan with a desire to serve God in every aspect of my life and to live out my faith!

I then started to go on other mission trips to serve with the gifts of music and teaching that God had given to me. God then gave me a desire to take other Americans to the mission field, so He could show them what He had shown to me. So, we started our ministry for that purpose. On our very first mission trip to the Philippines in 2001, our host pastor asked if I would teach a workshop on church administration to help the many pastors that he oversaw. I taught a one hour workshop and he liked it so much he asked if I would come back the next year and teach on that topic for a whole week at his Bible School! I about choked. Sensing God was at work, though, I said yes, thinking I would just go to and get books others had written and put a course together for them.

Unfortunately, I discovered that most of the books in the US were designed for American churches and would not be very helpful for the Philippine pastors. Since I had committed to help him, I started to develop the needed training myself based upon my business experience, church leadership roles, and most importantly, the Bible! What came out of that was a training course we call *"Management for Church Leaders."* It was well received in that first training. But again, God had bigger plans. He subsequently led us to take this training to 78 nations and set up a network of 64 global trainers in 31 nations to also teach this training. This was never my idea, but obviously God's plan!

So why me? Couldn't God have chosen a more talented, experienced trainer to develop this training? I was a businessman with a marketing career. What did I know about developing a training curriculum for pastors? And yet God did choose me. What Paul wrote in **1st Corinthians 1:26** also applied to me. I am *"not wise by human standards"* and I am *"not influential"* either. But God still chose to use me. Why? I believe it was because I had a desire to serve Him, serve others, and made myself available to Him. I am truly ordinary, but God built an entire ministry for me. Since our beginning in 2001, our ministry has trained over 34,000 pastors and church leaders in those 78 nations! As the Apostle Paul said in **1 Corinthians 3:6**, *"I planted the seed, Apollos watered it, but God made it grow!"* And boy, did God ever make it grow!

So, what is God asking you to do for Him? In order to answer that question, there are four things I believe you must do:

First, <u>you must listen for His voice</u>. Too often the busyness of our lives and the enormous amount of communication we absorb every day crowds out God's voice. God has a plan for each of our lives and a desire to use each of us in His Plan of salvation for all people. We all have a role to play that is unique for each one of us. God has gifted each of us with gifts so that we will use them to lift up the Body of Christ (**1 Corinthians 12:7**). If we fail to hear His call, there is no one else that can fill that role as uniquely as we can. So, we must clear away all the distractions and spend time in prayer so that we can hear Him. God was not getting my attention so He called me to Kazakhstan so He could!!

Secondly, <u>you must be willing to obey the call He gives to you</u>, regardless of your inadequacies or personal desires. God will often call us to something that we have no ability to do ourselves so that He can guide us and empower us by His Spirit (**Zechariah 4:6**). You see, if we can accomplish a goal all by ourselves then we do not need God's help. That's not how God works. He wants to participate with us and He wants us to rely on Him and not ourselves! And when we submit our lives to Him and His call God will use us to do some pretty amazing things that we could never do on our own! Our ministry is a testimony to that truth!

Third, <u>you must seek His counsel</u> (**1 Kings 22:5**). God doesn't call us to something and then abandon us. He waits patiently for us to come to Him to seek His advice and power to accomplish what He has given to us to do. Just as Jesus made Himself readily available to his disciples, God makes Himself readily available to us every moment through His Holy Spirit. All we need to do is pray and ask God and He will supply our needs (**Matthew 7:8**).

Fourth, <u>you must trust Him completely</u> (**Psalm 37:5**). To fulfil our calling, we must always look to God for guidance and avoid the temptation to "*do it ourselves*" or rely on our own wisdom or experience. Failure to trust in God and His ways will always lead us down a path of ruin or disappointment. We are not smart enough to have all the answers. But God is! The only way to measure our faith in God is to measure how much we trust Him!

So why does God use ordinary people like you and me to be a part of His Plan? Is it because we need something to do? Is it because we are more likely to be obedient? Is it because we know how to ask for directions? No. <u>God uses ordinary people so that God gets the glory!</u> (**1 Corinthians 1:29**) Ordinary people do not boast in themselves or their accomplishments. They boast in what God has done. On the contrary, famous or self-serving people often draw more attention to themselves than God. By lifting themselves up they actually block others from seeing God! God is a jealous God (**Exodus 20:5**) and he wants our undivided attention and worship. Not because He demands it, but because He alone is worthy of it!

Hudson Taylor, a well-known British missionary to China, said, *"God's work done in God's way will never lack God's supply."* I have seen God provide for our ministry in so many ways over the years. He has provided for us financially. He has protected us from harm when we travel. He has sent people to help us meet our needs. He has guided us through difficult times. And He often came through at the last minute, after we had done all that we could think of ourselves. God knows what we need before we speak it (**Romans 8:26**) and He longs to meet our needs (**Philippians 4:19**). God will equip us wherever we go when we go in His name and in His power! The Bible says it this way, *"Commit to the Lord whatever you do, and your plans will succeed."* (**Proverbs 16:3**)

God indeed uses ordinary people like you and me to do extraordinary things. Whether it's feeding the homeless, teaching children, going on mission trips, or simply sharing our faith with those we meet, by living out our faith God can produce amazing outcomes if we just let Him use us! Most of the things that we do for Him go unnoticed by the world. And we may never get to see the results of the things we do for Him in our lifetime either. But God sees them! And that's all that matters.

Because it's not about what we do, but all about what He does!

YOU ARE NOT STUCK!

Rev. Dr. Zenobia Bereal

*There hath no temptation taken you, but such as is common to man: but **God is faithful**, who will not suffer you to be tempted above that ye are able; but will with the temptation also **make a way to escape**, that ye may be able to bear it.*

Egyptians Are Chasing Me!

Have you ever seen "The Prince of Egypt" (an animated film by Dream Works)? The movie is an adaptation of the biblical story of Israel's miraculous exodus out of Egypt. God literally and supernaturally released them from slavery's iron grip! Relief flooded my soul as I watched Israel's jubilant, bold exodus. After much harsh persuasion from God, Pharaoh finally threw in the towel, and let God's people go!

No sooner had Israel made a clean get away from Egypt, they ran smack into the Red Sea! Now, I'm feeling exhausted, but the story gets even worse! To their extreme dismay, Israel saw Pharaoh and his army furiously in pursuit; he wanted revenge! They were overwhelmed. Panic and woe, doom and gloom set in! Did God betray Israel? Pharaoh behind and the Red Sea in front. Israel appeared to be stuck!

I did say the movie was an adaptation. By no means was Israel stuck in a deadly situation. Reading scripture clarifies that initially God spoke directly to Moses: *"GOD*

13

spoke to Moses: "Tell the Israelites to turn around and make camp at Pi Hahiroth, between Migdol and the sea. Camp on the shore of the sea opposite Baal Zephon. Pharaoh will think, 'The Israelites are lost; they're confused. The wilderness has closed in on them.' Then I'll make Pharaoh's heart stubborn again and he'll chase after them. And I'll use Pharaoh and his army to put my Glory on display. Then the Egyptians will realize that I am GOD. And that's what happened." Exodus 14:1-4

God declares, "... I am God". This is an introduction, a lesson, revelation, information, and declaration to Israel and Egypt, that God has taken over Israel's plight, so everyone and everything will fall in line. The entire situation was a Divine set up for further display of God's Glory! God knew it, and He told Moses, but Israel and the Egyptians had no idea they were both in for big surprises.

The moment terrified Israel who saw Egypt chasing after them as they cried out to God. Poor Moses was in the middle of the whole mess, and Israel blamed him for their predicament: *"Weren't the cemeteries large enough in Egypt so that you had to take us out here in the wilderness to die? What have you done to us, taking us out of Egypt? Back in Egypt didn't we tell you this would happen? Didn't we tell you, 'Leave us alone here in Egypt—we're better off as slaves in Egypt than as corpses in the wilderness.'"* Exodus 14:

Moses understood why Israel believed they were stuck, but even if he told them that God had set the whole thing up, they would not have believed him.

Circumstances were just too compelling. Israel's confidence was at an all-time low.

Fear has a way of dominating thoughts. The fact that God had miraculously freed them, after imposing ten plagues on Egypt, was not enough to give them faith in God nor Moses. Egypt had bullied Israel for so long, they developed slave mentalities. Sadly, Israel expressed that they were "*better off as slaves in Egypt than corpses in the wilderness*". Undoubtedly Moses thought to himself, ". . . but God just proved to us that He is with us, why are you doubting Him now? Besides, God has already let me know what is going to happen, and I BELIEVE GOD!"

Belief is the determining factor for walking in freedom or slavery. Israel *believed* slavery was better than facing freedom's challenges. Did you know that freedom is not free?` Instead of courageously believing Truth, people succumb to fear, living in self-deception and sin's bondage. This happens often.

Years ago, I had a friend who married a man that she did not love. She did it because it was economically convenient; she used her husband as a "meal ticket". He said he loved her, but as years passed, he turned out to be someone other than she expected. For the sake of autonomy, I will call my friends: "Sheila" and "Tom".

Sheila and Tom

Sheila was raised to be sincere and truthful. Although her mother passed away giving birth to Sheila, she was blessed to be raised by a loving father who would do anything for her. Sheila accepted Christ when she turned eighteen, under her father's ministry, who was a man full of integrity and grace. She really loved the Lord and her father. They both served God in the church, side by side. At twenty-one, Sheila completed her under graduate studies, and decided to take the LSAT because she wanted to go to law school. Life was really good.

Tragically, one day Sheila and her dad drove into a busy intersection, and a drunk driver plowed straight into the driver's side of the car! Sheila's dad was driving. He died on impact. Sheila's injuries were only minor. Immediately life flipped! Life can unexpectedly change on a dime. Sheila's did.

To Sheila's dismay, her father was not financially prepared for burial. Graciously, her family pitched in, and saved the day; however, for the first time in Sheila's life, she began to struggle to pay rent. All of her life she had depended on dad, but now in a flash, her faithful breadwinner was gone! He made it look so easy; why was it so hard? It was difficult because unbeknownst to Sheila, dad lived paycheck to paycheck, as so many people do; his financial struggles and suffering silently happened. Sheila had earned a full academic scholarship and worked her way through college, so she did not reach out to dad for help. However, nothing could have prepared her for the extreme changes dad's early tragic death would reveal!

Needless to say, Sheila's plans for taking the LSAT got totally derailed. Instead, she began working two part time jobs, while applying for full time work. Unfortunately, her bills totaled more than she could afford to pay, and Sheila began slowly but surely sinking into a financial abyss. Grief grew even more complex. She mourned the tragic loss of her father. Completely unaware, Sheila grieved the loss of her lifestyle, future, dreams. She was outraged about the reckless manner that all of it happened – by a drunk driver! This was outrageous! Where was God when she needed Him most? Silent. Admittedly, ever since dad died, Sheila had not even considered going back to church. It was not the same without him. Sheila was secretly mad at God for letting her dad die through the carelessness of a drunk driver. Yes, she blamed God.

One early Saturday morning Sheila received a phone call from Tom, an acquaintance who also attended her church. Tom wanted to check on her, because he missed seeing her at church. Sheila was surprised because she honestly thought Tom to be a nice guy, but unappealing. He acted quiet and shy, and always seemed to walk with his head down like he had low self-esteem. Sheila politely thanked Tom for calling but was shocked when he asked if he could drop by to give her a gift he'd purchased to lift her spirits. Without thinking too much about it, Sheila said "sure Tom, come on by".

During his visit Tom noticed Sheila had real needs. He offered to help out in any way he could, and Sheila let him do just that. After about a year's time, they were exchanging vows, saying "I do". The first few years of marriage were basically okay, routine, safe; needs were met, and life moved forward fast, without dad. Sheila and Tom went back to church. She worked for various auxiliaries, and Tom served in finances and administration.

After four years, Sheila grew tired and bored with her lifestyle. Although, she really was unhappy, she kept up the routine because it was financially convenient. Tom was as routine as the days of the week, but at the same time, he was also such a mystery. There was a weird "gap" in his personality that Sheila could not put her finger on. They never had kids, which made things easier for both of them. She tolerated Tom, worked a mundane job as a legal assistant, and attended church. Tom was a CPA, living on the surface as one person, and in the "gap" as another. He pleased his wife as best he could, even though he was a robotic, emotionally unavailable man. Sheila had learned how to please herself with pornography and toys in college. She had to maintain an image of being a good church girl. Life with Tom was no big deal. Instead of complaining, she just went back to what she'd already been doing in the past and ignored the Truth constantly staring her in the face.

The Truth is: Tom lived a double life. He was careful to avoid making waves by complaining or arguing at home. Instead he kept up the marriage routine, pleased his wife as much as possible, and saw men on the side whenever convenient. Tom lived "down low". Whenever Sheila worked late, he called "a friend". If she went on church trips, visited family, or spent time with the girls Tom would fill in the time "gap" by seeing his friend(s). Neither Tom nor Sheila had courage to confront the fact that they lived as slaves to self-deception and self-betrayal; sin. Sheila lived numb to the grief over her father's sudden death, coupled with the unforeseen financial crises that came with it. Tom lived numb from suffering sexual trauma by his uncle for six years straight. His mother was a single mom who believed he needed a father figure in his life, so she trusted her brother with surrogacy. Both people learned to self-medicate, coping with additive behaviors. They settled into living a lie, because freedom required honesty, and that price was just too high.

Like Israel, Sheila and Tom saw themselves as victimized slaves, stuck in life's dire circumstances that were so compelling they couldn't see past them. The Egyptians had bullied Israel for so long, their self-confidence and identities were severely damaged. Sheila and Tom suffered from life's brutalities, believing themselves to be stuck in overwhelming circumstances; so were also robbed of self-confidence and authenticity. All believed they were subject to negative realities because they believed they were slaves.

God is Able; Not You; Don't Panic!

Although it is often soon forgotten, especially under duress, God's children are exceptional. God takes ownership in a particular way. This does not mean His children don't experience hardship. In fact, God's children are assured they will suffer persecution, trials and tribulations. The difference is, God controls the "bigger picture". To see this, studying His Word is imperative! Study is accomplished by: listening to sermons, reading the bible, rehearsing and memorizing scripture, meditation, fellowship with believers in holy conversation, etc. To know God is to know oneself. Once your identity is established, your responses to trauma will reveal supernatural confidence. With your Spiritual mind, you will see past trauma, exercise faith in God, and ultimately triumph over defeated enemies. God fights your enemies, you fight the Good fight of faith! With God on your side, you are never stuck! Three truths are clear here: 1) God is in the driver's seat; 2) He's a covenant keeping God; and 3) your enemy is toast! God will make a "way of escape". Freedom is better.

THE DISCONNECT
LeeAnne Dyck

I work with children who have disabilities. It isn't what I planned when I graduated from school, but it is where I ended up through circumstances and the hand of God. I've worked in a program setting with children with severe autism and worked in the school system with children with various diagnosis from Fragile X to cerebral palsy. I have also run a private business for many years tutoring, coaching and teaching life skills to children with disabilities from Down syndrome to Asperger's. I don't mention this because I am looking for work because the needs are endless.

Whether I stared working with the family when their child was three or twelve, and regardless of nationality or religion, every mother said to me, "My child is broken." These mothers are universally without hope and resigned to the prospect of forever being caregivers. The dreams and hopes they possessed when they carried their children lay shattered in pieces smaller than dust.

Most blame themselves and say, "I must have done something to deserve this." Or, "I must have done something evil in a previous life." Somehow, we see God as an angry judge, not only ready to dole out punishment, but also dealing out lifelong hardship to make us pay for our sin, or the sin of an ancestor. Because of bad teaching, many Christians believe this. They have become so sin conscious that they believe they deserve every bad thing that happens.

Now I am not promoting sin or excusing it. Things we do can have devastating consequences. Unfortunately, often we give a nod to the idea that God loves us but, in our hearts, we believe that God is angry with us. We see Him like an angry father ready to take His fury out on us. If not that, we see God as measuring out punishment to keep us forever repenting and trying to earn his favor through our giving, service to others, and time spent reading the Bible and praying. You'll know this is you if you ever started a prayer by saying, "I am sorry I did not do more..."

A few years ago, I worked in a situation where my co-worker was a bully. Every day she found ways to put me down. She continually let me know that I did not measure up. I tried to please her and worked harder and harder, but I always fell short. I found myself continually apologizing to her. My conversations sounded like some of my prayers, "I am sorry I did not do more..." I spent my days in dread. Talking to her seemed like walking on eggshells because I never knew when she would make me pay for something I did or didn't do. She acted like I had a "hurt me" sign taped to my back. The longer I worked with her, the more I thought I deserved what she doled out.

Our Heavenly Father is not a bully. Jesus came to reveal His father as a God of love. He came to make a way for His father to become our father. Jesus told a story of a son who demanded his inheritance, then squandered it, and yet his father waited for him to return. When the son finally came back home, the father did not make him pay or treat him as less than a well-loved son.

I always felt a little jealous of the prodigal son because his father demonstrated love. My experience growing up didn't include unconditional love. My father doled out judgement whether I deserved it or not. I paid the price if my brothers misbehaved. He took it out on me if he had a bad day at work. So, in my head, I gave ascent that the Heavenly Father is loving and forgiving, but loving and forgiving to the lucky ones, and I wasn't one of those. I guess this is why I let people bully me. I grew up believing I deserved abuse.

People with children with disabilities don't see themselves as lucky, either. Often, they believe the lie that God is punishing them. However, soon they ask the questions, "What did my child do to deserve this?" and "Why is God punishing my child?" Even when we believe God is just in punishing us, we still have a hard time accepting a just God would make innocent children pay. We have a hard time reconciling a loving God being unloving towards us. This results in a spiritual disconnect.

When this disconnect happens, some people throw God out the window. They say things like, "I'll never measure up so why try." "God has abandoned me." "I can't go on pretending everything is fine when I am in church." "God loves the lucky ones. He doesn't love me." Or, "God hates me." Some say, "There can't be a God, when all these bad things happen."

I get that. I grew up going to church. Every day my father read the Bible at the table for family devotions after supper, and yet I wished I had a different father. A huge gulf existed between what he said and what I saw, so I grew up in a Christian family believing God hated me. I saw God based on my earthly father. When I left home, my father told me I was no longer his daughter and not to bother coming back. My father read the Bible every day and yet only saw God as a God of wrath. He portrayed God the way he understood God.

Since I left home, I learned that bad things happen to bad people. Bad things happen to mostly bad people. Bad things happen to somewhat good people and also to amazingly wonderful people. "If God isn't judging me, why is my child broken?" you ask. I could tell you it is because of bad luck or bad genetics. And we can blame the bad luck and bad genetics on polluted water or lack of nutritional value in our food or the side-effects of medication. We can blame trauma in the womb or during birth. Instead, I tell people we live in a fallen world. We are all damaged spiritually, emotionally and physically.

When I read in the Gospels of parents bringing their children to Jesus for Him to lay hands on them, I don't picture happy smiling parents bringing playful children. I picture the desperate and broken families I worked with over the years. And Jesus says to them, "The kingdom of heaven is made of your children and children just like them. Raising them isn't your cross to bear because I already paid the price when I went to the cross. Raising these who are most precious to me is the highest honor I can bestow."

Needless to say, after I left home I discovered the love and grace of Jesus, so I stopped seeing Father God as an extension of my own father. I am happy to tell you I had the privilege of introducing my Dad to the love of God. He became a different man and we became close friends. We reconnected with each other and with God.

Gary

My father was a great dad, yet I promised myself I would never be like him. My dad took me hunting and fishing. In the summer, I spent days with him at his work. He took the family camping and on road trips to see new places. He laughed freely and told funny stories that had everyone in stiches. He was one of the most compassionate men I ever met. Now I do want my children saying all of those things about me, however, my father was broken, and that had an effect on me.

The doctor diagnosed my father with leukemia when he was fifty-years old, but my father was ill from the time he turned fifteen. He got terrible headaches where the dimmest light hurt his head and every noise sounded like someone banging a bass drum. In my growing up years, he spent a lot of time in a dark room trying to sleep off the migraine and I spent a lot of time outside, preferably nowhere close to home.

I didn't know it at the time, but I learned to see God like my dad. When God spent time with me, nothing could be better. Then there were times where I shouldn't bother God. He wasn't available. My little trouble or my recent discovery wasn't something I should talk to him about. It seemed like a large do-not-disturb sign stood between me and my Heavenly Father. After a while, I prayed only in emergencies.

I'm not blaming my father for having leukemia. When he was a teenager, a doctor said to his parents, "Your son has a very square jawbone. We have a medical miracle that can fix that, so he looks normal." As my grandparents did not want their son called abnormal, they said yes to treatment. The doctor shot radiation into either side of my father's jaw until the bone shrunk. The radiation reshaped my father's jaw while it destroyed his bone marrow. Soon afterward, he began having headaches, a symptom of the disease that eventually took his life.

In a lot of ways my father acted like his father although, like me, he probably swore to do better. For example, when I was a child my father never told me, "I love you." I heard those words for the first time when I was 31 and my father and I were in the middle of an argument. It came out something like this, "I don't agree with what you are doing, but I still love you." Those words floored me. He actually said he loved me. Before LeeAnne and I had children, I told her that I would say those words to our children every chance I got. I asked my father sometime later why he never told me he loved me. He answered, "You are just supposed to know. My father never said those words to me, so I never said them to you."

I saw God like my dad. He loved me, and I was supposed to know it. However, my father never gave direct compliments either.

Apparently, he feared compliments would fill his children with pride. Instead, when I did something good, my father would tell my brother, "Gary did such a great job. I am so proud of him." My father often told me me how happy he felt with my brother's accomplishments. I'm sure my brother hated me because he thought Dad loved me and not him. And I tried and tried to please my father, but I knew he only loved my brother. So, I believed God loved me a little. After all, I was his child, but he loved my brothers and sisters more.

Then God broke into my life with multiple miracles, signs and wonders and shattered my misconceptions of Father God's love for me. Although I promised I would never be like my father, I discovered I really only wanted to be more like my Papa God.

The doctor gave my dad five years to live when they found the cancer, but my father lived more than twenty more years. In that time, he told me many times that he loved me. And my children heard those words from him, too. Not everyone gets the disconnects in their lives repaired, but we can take Jesus at His Word. His Father is our Father, and He loves us.

Gary and LeeAnne Dyck are co-authors of *Miracles: Your impossible is Possible*

Gary Dyck is author of *Bears, Bobsleds and Other Misadventures* *www.GaryDyck.com*

ELEMENTARY
Gloria Pierre Dean

Before me, I see a room full of pink, brown and yellow faces, clad in black, red and brown shirts, with straight and curly, long and short tresses.

Each child is so utterly unique, wearing the "'coded" uniforms and they are all the "loved" of a parent or two.

They are a visual array of God's created humanity and the hope for the future of this country. Elementary students, they are called, and with feet poised on the edge of mid-youth immaturity, they are leaving childhood behind as they climb in and out of schools' transports systems and parents' cars.

Each one exhibiting similar behavior patterns, yet unique and beautiful. They are made in God's image.

Suzi sits compliant and strangely quiet; so easy to teach while Joss, like some others, is openly non-compliant, troublesome, loud, difficult to teach and yet unforgettable.

In a system held together by rules and rule enforcers of whom I am one, they are housed in safe buildings designed for easy access yet encircled by iron fences, in a culture rife with gun violence.

The purpose is for learning not only from books but from each other. Like native multi-colored wildflowers in early bloom in a garden planted and tended by God's creation, are the children. They must grow strong. I love that the multi-racial mix, it spells hope for harmony in the future.

Adult male and female teachers find their purpose in this milieu. Big-hearted, kind and strong, giving love and sowing legacy seeds into the future.

Many provide meals and clothes anonymously. We call ourselves teachers and assistant teachers, but we are students too.

"Lord Jesus," I pray, "keep my heart soft and help me to love even the difficult ones."

As I walk by the clinic I see her again. Last week it was her arm, on Monday it was her finger and today her knee... I ask myself, what is causing this beautiful child to be "ill"? What is the underlying cause of the flow of sickness. Could it be a manifestation of a deeper problem?

God knows what it is; so, I pray, not only for her but for each one because I know that I was placed here for a God-given purpose.

Jesus said, "Love your neighbors as you love yourself." {Mark 12:31}

Time to sew and spread His love, in humility and using the tools of the Holy Spirit.

Next year they will transition to middle school. On the threshold of adulthood, I hope they make a difference and thrive, and not only academically.

When I see them away from their desks doing non-academics, I realize how gifted many of them are. 'A' student in mathematics, science and history amaze me. Dancers twirl on the floor, artists exhibit hand-crafted items and, athletes fly on winged feet across managed fields. Proud parents visit on viewing days and watch with smiles as their "babies" excel and "show off" for us all.

As I watch, my mind reflects on the Words of the Lord in Psalms:

" *Behold, children are a heritage from the LORD, the fruit of the womb a reward. Like arrows in the hand of a warrior are the children of one's youth. {Psalm 127:3-4}*"

The revelation that many of the children are from broken homes does not surprise me. Stories of drug addicted, or imprisoned parents reach deep into my heart, and I pray for the Lord to help them and keep them safe. An example is a beautiful girl called Marigold.

Her mother came to the 5th grade school concert and I saw such shame on her face. She avoided looking at her mother. I went over to introduce myself and I smelt the drugs on her clothes and her hair. So now I knew why she had sad eyes, was often late for school and wore the same stained pants each day.

The school is a place for beautiful friendships and partnering with others. On game day they are all smiles as they intermingle with beaming faces.

Finally, but not of less importance is the lack of the spiritual that I see in what they are taught. God, the Bible and Creation are not mentioned. The Word of God says that we should "train up a child in the way he should go" {Proverbs 22:6}; the question in my heart is - are we planning for a nation of atheists?

I know that many may already go to church, but what about the ones who do not? As I walk the grounds and stay off the grass, I pray for "His Kingdom to come" in our nation and schools.

{My article is based on impressions formed while working in a local elementary school. Any names are changed but all else is factual.}

A MAN OF THE MOMENT

Hazel E. Pinder

God, the author of creation, sat watching the world. It was in a gigantic mess through the peoples' wilfulness. The people, wayward in their actions and lifestyle, had forgotten their roots. The land was in mayhem, snared by the Philistines, a pagan nation in Canaan, who ruled them.

The Lord God sighed and sent angels out to search for a man who he could use to free His people. It was a difficult task, for most men were engulfed in their own pursuits, and few had the caliber that was required. There was one possibility, which had caught the Lord God's attention, an old couple longing for a child, who could not conceive.

Always one step ahead of everyone, the Lord God asked His angel to visit her with a message. She was the wife of Manoah, a Hebrew man of Zorah. To the great surprise of the couple, the angel of God arrived and informed her of the Lord's plans for the future and came back on another visit to see her husband.

The angel announced the great news, that they would have a son, who was to be brought up as a Nazirite and that he would bring deliverance to the nation. As a leader there was also a special dispensation for him; because the Lord was going to use him during his lifetime.

The Lord endowed Samson with incredible strength, which lay in his long hair; a fantastic gift, although he was to become a very controversial leader.

There is no doubt, Samson's lifestyle was confusing, which is why the story of this extraordinary man, a judge in the land, is difficult to understand.

Being nurtured as a Nazirite, you'd expect the life of this Hebrew leader to be an excellent example of holiness. Indeed, it seems to be in the beginning.

Instead, the opposite happens, and his life becomes a mixture of unruliness and lust. The man's lifestyle typifies a wilful teenager, set on "having his own way" and not concerned for anyone else. He flouts tradition, bullies his parents and always chooses to live in an unholy way, seemingly opposite to the Lord's way.

The whole story seems one of absolute disappointment, a tale of disillusion for those watching on, as his parents tried to cope with this wilful character. His choice of women and lustful spirit, plus his total disregard for the traditions laid down for his people, made everyone gasp with shame.

Although as you read his life story, this is the way God had planned everything.

Lustful and arrogant, Samson eventually became infatuated with a Philistine woman, which was opposite to all that his parents wanted.

A wedding ensued and then a saga of disappointment for him, as she betrayed his confidence. Through this, a considerable confrontation developed, and Samson killed thirty Philistines.

He was soon to find an even worse scenario confronting him when he found out that another man had taken his new wife! Furious he retaliated, setting fire to the Philistine's wheat and olive groves, by using three hundred foxes, with firebrands to their tails.

His actions provoked the fierce anger of the Philistines, who didn't take long to quickly responded by murdering his wife and father-in-law. Incensed once again, he went out and killed many Philistines. It was typical of the events all through Samson's life.

The Philistines desperate by now to apprehend Samson, cunningly tried to manipulate the Hebrews, into giving Samson to them. Three thousand Hebrews arrived where he was, fearful of not obeying the will of their rulers, the Philistines. Quite wise to the strategy of the Philistines, Samson yielded to the ploy and allowed the Hebrews to tie him up. Tied up seemingly a prisoner, he waited for the enemies of his people to arrive, and when they came to capture him, he broke free and chased after them.

Angered by their audacity in using his people to try and capture him, he then made a move, showing his power. With his mighty strength, he used a fresh jawbone from a donkey to attack and kill a thousand of them.

He had become notoriety, because of his strength and behavior, possibly if he'd lived in this century, we might have called him a 'hot-headed' man, who lived above the law. Furious about losing his wife, he went to Gaza and made a rendezvous with a woman of ill-repute.

It wasn't long before the locals surrounded the house; trying to capture him, annoyed at his audacity. Samson fooled them, escaped and mocked them by taking away the city gates and leaving them forty miles away. It was humiliating for the city of Gaza, and they were out for revenge.

Realizing that Samson was a judge, a ruler of the land, who somehow doesn't fit into "the box" as a holy man, is difficult to come to terms with for many people.

Quite soon, this notorious rebel raiser fell in love again with a Philistine woman named Delilah. From the commencement of their relationship, Delilah manipulated it. The Philistines eager to snare Samson made her a lucrative deal. She was treacherous, very beguiling and full of betrayal.

"Discover the secret of Samson's strength, reveal it to us, and we will reward you with much silver," was their cunning ploy.

Of course, beguiled by a beautiful woman, Samson was a ready target for all kinds of deceit that Delilah presented, while her nagging and pleading to know the reason for his strength was continuous. Samson eventually gave in and told her about the Lord's anointing, and quickly she alerted the authorities, while he was asleep.

The Philistines hidden, came quickly to overpower Samson after Delilah cut off his hair. They were ecstatic that at last, they had captured this troublesome leader. Samson weak, could not fight them as his power and strength had gone. It was all so easy, once his hair was gone, his anointing had ceased, and he became a man dependant on his strength, without the Lord's anointing. Weak and overpowered by the soldiers, he was shackled, blinded and ridiculed; the Philistines were victorious.

It was a massive humiliation for the Israelites, their leader captured. On the face of it, the story and life of Samson seem to be finished, ending up as a failure.

Once he became a prisoner of the Philistines, the hope of the Hebrew nation was gone. The Lord had let him go, and this wayward man spent his days grinding in prison, contemplating his future.

Alone shackled, contemplative, he didn't forget who he served and that the Lord was his keeper, although he also knew of his misdemeanors. Samson, the Lord's mighty man who was poised to save the nation, what had happened?

A question we may ask ourselves, is this how leaders are to behave, recognizing, of course, it is not, but the Lord had chosen him? In this circumstance as in all situations God is in control; He is the winner, and His timing is perfect!

After some time, a day came, when the Philistines had a festival to sacrifice to their God Dagon and brought out Samson to be ridiculed at the temple. Three thousand were above him on the roof and hundreds more where he stood in the temple. Standing in a central place, he asked for his arms to be shown the central pillars, so he could hold on to them. His hair had grown, but he looked as a diminished shackled figure after his time incarcerated.

The Philistines intent on worshipping their god taunted him, congratulating themselves on capturing Samson. Blind, encased in darkness, Samson was on his own, completely shut-off from everything, but in this place of singlemindedness, he called out to his God.

The Lord had a plan for this wilful man; he wasn't forgotten, and it was to be enacted out at this time. Calling on the Lord Yahweh to come, to give him power and strength, for this one significant act that he was to perform. Samson held on to the pillars, willing to be used for the deliverance of Israel, in this final act of courage, his expression of faith.

The Lord gave Samson the strength that he required, and he gripped the pillars, and with a mighty shout to the Lord, the building came down. A man like no other leader, flawed and finally broken, but still the Lord's man, knowing to whom he belonged. With this one mighty act, many were killed as the pillars gave way, the roof caved in, and over three thousand Philistines died. Samson achieved it all for his God. He had saved the Hebrew nation; it was a victory.

I realize many believe Samson's story is pure fantasy, and it may be, but the Bible is the inspired Word of God. Leaders are accountable to the Lord, for all their actions. As a leader, we may consider that Samson fell short of being the best, but the Lord had chosen him. We stumble in our minds often over the way God does things. Is this not like our leaders today, sometimes we are dubious in the way they do things, but have we the right to pull them down in gossip? Yes, we can graciously confront them when they are not declaring the Lord's word, but we must be cautious even then. Our calling, whatever our position in the church, is to pray. Leadership falls into so many categories, while we all have a responsibility to be ready to be used by God, weak as we are, our strength is in our God, the Potter, for we are just clay.

"But he knoweth the way that I take: when he hath tried me, I shall come forth as gold." (Job 23:10)

Leadership is a gift of service, a laying down of our will, and doing things by the Lord's anointing, not our own. Many have been chosen for "such a time as this," for possibly just a moment in their life when God uses them.

A photograph that always resonates with me, reminding me of this fact, is one I saw in the Holocaust museum in Israel. In the picture, a grandfather walks to the gas chamber, with a long line each side of him, of many

many small Jewish children holding on to each other's hand. He led them with a smile as they all walked singing. To me he seemed to be, "A man for the moment", giving reassurance to those tiny ones, at the time of their need. Not thinking of himself but living and loving them through the situation for that dreadful for them in their lives.

A lesson indeed to be ready, for whatever we are called to do, and to do it as best we can, with God's hand upon us.

Hazel E Pinder
Author "Cyronus and the Treasures of the Kingdom"
'The Promise of Heaven"

SHOWING A MINISTRY OF PRESENCE

Jessie Glover Wilson

There are some things in life that we find difficult to do and the focus of this writing is to bring to our attention to those times when we need to engage in a ministry of presence. Such times are in consoling those in grief, those who are homebound due to disabilities, and those who are burdened with being the responsibility for care of a loved one. We refer to the one needing care as the care receiver, and the one giving the care as the caregiver, or caretaker.

Certainly, we know these are difficult situations and, though, we would like to avoid the role of a consoler for fear of saying or doing the wrong thing, it behooves us to do so as Scripture gives us the authority and makes it duty to do so. We may not all have the gift of mercy, but it does take compassion. In fact , I John 3:17 states that anyone who, "… seeth his brother in need, and shutteth up his bowels of compassion from him, how dwelleth the love of God in him?" Our concern for others does matter to the Lord as it is a powerful witness to those of the world. When we partner with the Lord in this ministry, others are able to experience God's presence through us. This is so awesome!

The role of a consoler to someone who had lost a loved one may be the most difficult role for us. Please understand your presence, even if you just say nothing but smile, squeeze a hand or a shoulder, speaks volume to griever. It says to the grieving, you are not alone, we are here for you, we hurt with you and, we care.

A wrong way is illustrated by how Job was ministered to by his three friends. For seven days they sat with him, wore sack cloth and mourned with him saying not a word. It would have been well if they had left after that, but they stayed and instead of saying helpful words of comfort to him, they poured condemnation upon him. All they had to offer was judgmentalism. In a time of grief who needs such friends? Most of us would not follow such an example. But there are clichés that we might avoid such as, "God knows best or, all things work together for good, or they are better off." I remember so clearly sixteen years ago, standing at the crib of my granddaughter, taking my turn spending time with her as we were told by the doctor that she had twenty-four hours to live. A very sweet nurse whispered in my ear, "You know God loves her more and will take care of her better than we." I was not in the mood to hear those words. I wanted to say, "But I want to have a chance to love her and hold her and rock her". She meant well, though.

It is true, culture plays a big part in how we mourn. Some eastern countries show great outpouring of weeping and even beating and injuring themselves with ropes, etc. Our own country has changed grieving practices as the wearing of black for a year. I remember my uncle who regularly went around and sat with relatives and the body all night. Visitation times have replaced the all-night wakes for the most part.

The immediate hours and days after the death are very busy for the family. They function in a state shock and are dazed but keep going forward, as plans for the funeral and burial have to be completed. The funeral is, of course, stressing but in all of this, usually many people are around offering help wherever they can. Then comes the hard part. After a week or two have passed, the husband or wife, and or family, as it may be, suddenly have to face life without the loved one, and often find an aloneness and quietness that are deafening.

The taking care of business matters that follow the burial may keep minds occupied, for a while, but at some point, the grieving process will become more apparent and, we the friends, have all returned to our normal lives. No, we cannot stay around and hold hands, but we can make calls, send cards, and offer help and just keep in touch.

The church family has an obligation to continue ministering to those in grief for as long as it takes. This should be done by ministerial calls, Sunday School Classmates, visits by grief support group personnel and or Stephen ministers. Grief material is readily available for information on the grief process. Should the person be in need of further help, then, they may be referred to a grief support group, either one offered by the church or elsewhere in the community. This information is available online.

If we keep in mind that these are wounded souls in our midst, then we will not be guilty of "out of sight, out of mind" or what really is forgetfulness. As Christ would put it "as much as ye do this to one of these, ye do it unto me."

The need for those who are ill or disabled and are confined to home for a long period of time, or even those who are terminal present a great need for a ministry of presence. These persons are isolated, and loneliness is a big problem, as well as the probability of depression. Contact with friends is so important These care receivers still have feelings and needs. They need a familiar face, a touch, an encouraging word or a prayer. The psalmist David wrote "friends are a delight" and called them "excellent ones". Are we a delight to others? Friendship is able to lift others' spirits.

Lastly, those who are caretakers, especially over an extended time, and attention is not given to these persons, it can be lethal. A strong statement. Yes! As a nurse, I can vouch for the truth of this pronouncement. These individuals, generally, are a mate, another relative, or a hired caretaker. The stress of care taking over a period of time will take its toll if her/, his social, physical, emotional and spiritual needs are not met. Lack of socialization, neglect of proper care for self, and failure of others to intervene are all contributing factors to the fact that many caretakers, actually, die before the care receiver. It is one thing to be compassionate, but one may become consumed and not even notice one's health is slipping away. A ministry of presence can be soul saving and lifesaving!

Let us analyze other contributing factors that put a care giver at risk in this caring relationship. Many of these cases are those in which the care is needed, but cure is unlikely, or where life can be sustained for a long period of time. If the care giver is a loved one and death is the expected outcome, anticipatory grief can ensue, causing depression, or an insidious downward progression of the care giver's health.

The personalities of the two participants in this situation will determine the dynamics of this relationship. If the care receiver is difficult to care for and uses controlling, demanding and manipulative and other negative behaviors, and the care giver is unable to set boundaries, she/he has aided to one's own decline in health.

On the other hand, not all care givers are kind and gentle and, herein, lies the need for those outside visitors to be alert and intervene if necessary. Abuse of the care receiver and or abuse of the care giver does occur. One very important need for the care giver is that they get adequate rest. Truly, these individuals must have breaks. Help them search out community resources such as Visiting Angels, Hospice, and Home Health Agencies. Some churches have a Homebound ministry, and/ or a Stephen Ministry designed to see that regular visits are made to these homebound participants. It is for this reason that our ministry to these situations provides an objective outsider who will more likely be able to tell if intervention is warranted. We become advocates and instruments of

God's mercies and compassion. Are we not our brother's keeper?

I have found that another useful tool to use when visiting these homes is to follow the example of prayer as laid out in the book of James. Laying a hand on the shoulder, arm or holding the hand are discreet ways to give them human touch. Offering communion makes them feel a part of the church family, as well as giving them spiritual comfort. Do as the Holy Spirit leads for God is with you in this healing ministry.

As a nurse educator, I recall one of my newly graduated young nurses receiving news that she had a malignant tumor of her spinal cord. She went through chemo therapy and went back to work. To be a nurse had been her life's dream. As she was making rounds one evening, she came across a young man who was also facing cancer treatments. Jeannie took time to talk to him and he said to her," You don't have a clue as to how I feel?" These were the days when nurses wore caps. She looked at him with tears in her eyes, slowly reached up, took off her cap, and then her wig, displaying her balding head from her chemo therapy. They both wept for each other.

My dear ministering angels, do not fear when you are partnering with God in this ministry. You are never alone. The Holy Spirit will guide you in thoughts, words and actions. The beauty of human touch is indiscernible to put into words, but perhaps this will do, "It is all about Grace!"

I Desire to Be Like You, Lord!
It is my desire to be like You, Lord.
But to do this alone, I cannot do.
Help me to have love, to others will flow.

Humility and meekness, I surely must grow
Make me dear Lord, into what I should be
Give me a clear vision, to be able to see
Those who hurt and come my way

May I be willing to follow this day
Take my heart and make it like new

To help me be caring, kind and true
To those who are poor, and need a hand
Or those who are weak and cannot stand

Binding the wounds, with sweet caress
Freeing those in bondage, those in distress
Give me compassion, so I can share
With another's burden, those hard to bear

More like the Master, is my heart's plea
Christ at my side, partners, you see
Doing His work, and showing His love
From now, till He calls from above

Oh, to be like you Lord is my hearts prayer
Jessie Glover Wilson (2015)

Jessie Glover Wilson - Author: The Diploma Nurse; Her Shining Day-Her Fading Touch!
Beyond the Shadow of Grief
Articles for Authors for Christ

A CAN OF CREAMED CORN
Lynne Wells Walding

God hears and meets us where ever we are in our walk with Him.

What is a miracle?

A miracle is any event that occurs strictly because God willed it to occur. If the same or identical event occurs without God's intervention . . . it's a coincidence. Small miracles are often dismissed as coincidences because witnesses don't have the faith to believe.

Most Christians don't have any problem believing in Biblical miracles. Although some have doubts about modern-day miraculous events. But miracles still happen. Healings that defy reason. Financial windfalls from unexpected sources.

Yet, there are doubters.

A personal encounter with Jesus that affects only one individual is the hardest miracle to defend. If no other person experienced it, how can they be sure it happened? It could be the teller's over-active imagination. However, sometimes even the most skeptical critic has to admit . . . *this had to be from God.*

The following true story is one of those times . . .

as told to *Christian fiction author, Lynne Wells Walding*

* * *

Creamed corn oozed down the plaid wallpaper. Jagged pieces of my serving dish lay shattered on the floor. My five-year-old son's eyes were wide with fear.

And my husband of two years was bellowing. "I told you I *hate* creamed corn. I don't care *how much* the brat loves it. I don't want to look at it when I'm eating."

He shoved away from the table, and my heart faltered in my chest. *He's going to blame my little boy.* "I'm sorry." I stuttered. "It's my fault. I kind of had a taste for it today and I didn't think you'd mind."

Apparently satisfied with his tantrum and my quick apology, he pulled back to the table and continued eating as though nothing had happened, while I frantically cleaned up the mess. I'd almost earned my son another whipping. *I've got to be more careful,* I thought.

I'd only known him six weeks when we married. He seemed to be a decent fellow and I was desperate to give my three-year-old, fatherless son a real family that would include traditional family values. As a result of my haste, I'd plunged him into the worst kind of dysfunctional family. This evening was one of the few times we'd actually eaten a meal together. Since shortly after our wedding—on most days—my husband would stop for a drink on the way home from work. And he never quit at only one drink. To avoid constant criticism, or worse yet undeserved punishment, it was best for my son to be in bed asleep before he got home.

Aside from my time alone with my little one, my brightest moments in life were spent with my mother, who made the three-hour drive to visit for a few days once or twice a month. As an added bonus, my husband was always on his best behavior in Mother's presence. If she knew him better, she'd worry. So, I couldn't bring myself to tell her about his "other side."

She looked forward to baby-sitting her only grandchild at least once during a visit, while we took in a movie. And, oh, how she loved to grocery shop. We'd hit our favorite supermarket while the boy was in kindergarten and spend the entire morning roaming the aisles. Laughing, joking, and just being silly, like we always did when we were together—for as long as I could remember.

In an uncharacteristic, serious moment Mother gave me a stern mother/daughter look. "Why do you never buy creamed corn for him? You know how much he loves it."

"Oh, his dad doesn't like it, and it just sits in the pantry. I figure there are lots of other things they *both* like." Trying, as always, to paint a picture of family unity, referring to their relationship as father and son. A relationship that hadn't gelled.

Mother gave me a *that's not a very good excuse* kind of look but said no more.

When we were checking out, I noticed the cashier ringing up a can of creamed corn. "Wait," I asked, "where did that come from?"

The cashier paused and looked from one of us to the other. Mother was looking upward, humming a nameless little tune. I stifled a laugh and gave the cashier a nod to go ahead and ring up the corn. *Typical grandmother.* No words were ever exchanged about the can of creamed corn.

But when we got home from the grocery store, I hid the can behind other canned goods in the pantry with every intention of throwing it out when Mother went home. However, when my husband and I got home from the movies that evening, I looked for it and it was gone. I found it in the trash receptacle, empty and rinsed clean. *How sweet. Now they're both happy. He got his creamed corn. And Mother had the pleasure of doing something special for her grandson. With no one the wiser.*

From that day forward—for more than three years—whenever Mother and I shopped together, there would be a single can of creamed corn in the basket at checkout. Neither of us ever spoke of this little tradition. To put it into words would have been to spoil the sublimity. Yet, we'd share a smile as we put up the groceries, and she'd watched curiously as I carefully hid it behind other items. I often wondered if Mother instinctively knew more about my fractured family life than she let on.

The news of Mother's untimely death hit me hard. "I'm sorry to have to tell you this," her doctor mumbled, "but your mother is dead." Harsh, unfeeling words, spoken to a totally unprepared, loving daughter. He hadn't even asked if someone was there with me. Fortunately, I was not alone. And the enormity of my grief shocked my husband into good behavior.

For about two weeks.

* * *

"I want some ice cream." It was late, and he was drunk.

"We don't have any ice cream. I can make you some pudding." My stock of groceries was depleted because I hadn't felt like shopping. I had only recently accepted the Lord as my Savior. And though I'd tried, on Mother's last visit, to witness to her . . . I was afraid I'd failed miserably. Failed my mother. And failed the Lord.

Obscenities filled the air. "I don't want pudding. I want ice cream. And I want pie. And while you're at it get some . . . " He rattled off a list of things he wanted . . . now . . . not tomorrow or the next day.

I checked to be sure the little one was asleep and said a prayer that he'd not awaken before I got back. Unless provoked, my husband would most likely not leave his recliner before I got back. In fact, he'd probably be asleep and would have forgotten all about the ice cream and pie he was demanding.

At 11:00 p.m. the only grocery store in our neighborhood was closed. I had to drive quite a distance to a run-down part of town to find an all-night grocery store. Dull from years of neglect, a flickering neon sign in the window proclaimed the business was open. But the oppressing dimness inside seemed to say otherwise.

I was the only customer, pushing a battered buggy over buckled floors, as sagging shelves crammed with dust-covered cans seemed to be threatening imminent collapse. The only other person in the store was a small man of East Indian descent who was tending the cash register. I felt his dark eyes following me as I struggled up one aisle and down the other. And I tried in vain to hold back the tears that welled up in my eyes. It seemed all the weight of the world was resting on my shoulders. I'd been able to handle it all . . . until I lost Mother. Thinking she may have missed Heaven was the most painful idea I'd ever had to endure.

The tears came. My make-up, already smudged from a hard day's work, ran down my cheeks and, I'm sure, left black mascara streaks. And I knew my eyes had to be red and puffy. Even worse, I couldn't keep from audibly sobbing. I was pleading with the Lord, over and over, the same plea.

"Jesus, please give me a sign that she's with You. Jesus, please give me a sign that she's with You."

Not yet schooled enough in God's Word to know that Jesus doesn't dole out signs like Halloween candy, I kept asking for a sign. I tried to pray another way. I really did. But those were the only words that would come. *"Jesus, please give me a sign that she's with You."*

Finally, physically exhausted from shoving the buggy over the buckled floor, and emotionally drained from grief, I wrestled a nearly-full cart to the cash register and methodically placed each item on the counter. I couldn't help but recall all the times Mother and I had shopped together, laughing and cutting up. And of course, our little tradition, known only to the two of us . . . and Jesus. *No more creamed corn.* I vowed that little secret would stay with me until I met Jesus face-to-face.

Wordlessly, the cashier rang up each item, glancing up at me from time to time. He sacked the groceries as he rang them up. Two large paper sacks full. The only words he spoke were to tell me how much I owed.

I paid with cash and he gave me the change. Still no words were exchanged.

I turned to go and had only taken a couple of steps when the little man spoke. *"Come back,"* he said in broken English. *"I forget to geeve you someting."*

Reluctantly, and with a small twinge of fear at being alone with this stranger who'd been watching me so closely, I returned to the counter. Not turning around, but simply moving backwards a couple of steps.

I flinched when he reached under the counter, not knowing what to expect. But whatever it was he picked up, he placed in the top of the grocery bag closest to himself.

"I can't take something I didn't pay for." I objected, reaching to retrieve the object.

With his first seemingly mindful utterance, he made a shoving gesture toward me and chirped, "Leave! Go!" Scowling, he pointed to the door.

I got out of there as quickly as I could. My car was right outside the door under a lone streetlight. Anxious to get to a safer part of town, I threw the groceries on the front passenger seat and dashed around to the driver's side. Snapping the door locks even as I jumped in, I took off for familiar territory.

When I was within a few blocks of home, I stopped at my regular gas station, where I knew the attendants and felt safe. But I didn't stop for gas. I stopped to see what the strange little man had put in my grocery sack.

At that moment, Jesus and Mother must have been looking upward and humming a nameless little tune *together*. Because, with the assistance of one clueless little helper (or maybe he was an angel), they'd slipped something into my groceries.

A can of creamed corn.

Epilogue

Susan grew in her walk with the Lord. But attempting to win her husband with patience and kindness was futile. In time, knowing how much God cared for them, Susan gathered the courage to remove herself and her son from the physical and emotional abuse they'd endured for so long. God has blessed them beyond their dreams.

Lynne Wells Walding
Website: lynnewellswalding.com
Published works: Pastor McAlester's Bride
Winnoby Cabin
Ian's Song
The Trinity Quilts (due for release in August 2018)

WAS DONALD TRUMP APPOINTED BY GOD?
Michael Larson

The short answer to the question is, "Yes." But truly, all leaders are appointed by God. Leaders in all settings are set up by God. We find them in the home, at school, at work, and in government, both locally and nationally. Ultimately, all men are accountable unto God. God established the institution of government after Noah and his family stepped out of the Ark. Genesis 9:6 says, "Whoso sheddeth man's blood, by man shall his blood be shed: for in the image of God made he man." Human government was necessary because of man's sinful nature. God had to destroy the antediluvian generation, minus Noah and his family, because "every imagination of the thoughts of [man's] heart was only evil continually" (Genesis 6:5). Proverbs 21:1 says, "The king's heart is in the hand of the LORD, as the rivers of water: he turneth it whithersoever he will." Also, "...the throne is established by righteousness" (Proverbs 16:12). Daniel 2:21 says, "And [God] changeth the times and the seasons: he removeth kings, and setteth up kings..." Daniel also repeated three times that "the most High (God) ruleth in the kingdom of men, and giveth it to whomsoever he will" (4:17, 25, 32).

Although God appoints all leaders, not all leaders receive His blessings. The word "righteousness" in Proverbs 16:12 is referring to God's righteousness. There is no righteousness in man, except that which is imputed unto him by the shed blood of Jesus Christ when he becomes born again. All of our righteousnesses are as filthy rags (Isaiah 64:6).

Christians must not think of government as a man-made institution or as an institution bent on ruining God's will. The Bible tells us how our attitude should be towards government. Romans 13:1-7 says, "Let every soul be subject unto higher powers. For there is no power but of God: the powers that be are ordained of God. Whosoever therefore resisteth the power, resisteth the ordinance of God: and they that resist shall receive to themselves damnation. For rulers are not a terror of good works, but to the evil. Wilt thou then not be afraid of the power? do that which is good, and thou shalt have praise of the same: For he is the minister of God to thee for good. But if thou do that which is evil, be afraid; for he beareth not the sword in vain: for he is a minister of God, a revenger to execute wrath upon him that doeth evil. Wherefore ye must needs be subject, not only for wrath, but also for conscience sake. For this cause pay ye tribute also: for they are God's ministers, attending continually upon this very thing. Render therefore to all their dues: tribute to whom tribute is due; custom to whom custom; fear to whom fear; honour to whom honour." Also, "Submit yourselves to every ordinance of man for the Lord's sake: whether it be to the king, as supreme; Or unto governors, as unto them that are sent by him for the punishment of evildoers, and for the praise of them that do well. For so is the will of God, that with well doing ye may put to silence the ignorance of foolish men: As free, and not using your liberty for a cloke of maliciousness, but as the servants of

God. Honour all men. Love the brotherhood. Fear God. Honour the king. Servants be subject to your masters with all fear; not only to the good and gentle, but also to the froward. For this is thankworthy, if a man for conscience toward God endure grief, suffering wrongfully. For what glory is it, if, when ye be buffeted for your faults, ye shall take it patiently? but if, when ye do well, and suffer for it, ye take it patiently, this is acceptable with God" (1 Peter 2:13-20).

Some may ask, "But why would God appoint Donald Trump?" We can find the answer in 1 Corinthians 1:26-29: "For ye see your calling, brethren, how that not many wise men after the flesh, not many mighty, not many noble, are called: But God hath chosen the foolish things of the world to confound the wise; and God hath chosen the weak things of the world to confound the things which are mighty; And base things of the world, and things which are despised, hath God chosen, yea, and things which are not, to bring to nought things that are: That no flesh should glory in his presence." Some people think of Samson as a kind of bodybuilder-looking man, when he was probably a puny fellow that God decided to use to confound the Philistines (the mighty). Think of Moses, how he tried to tell God that he was unqualified. But God used him to lead about a million Jews out of Egypt to the Promised Land. God used Gideon, who the average person reading his account would deem him a coward. Here was a man hiding, yet God called him "a mighty man of valour." Think of how God used David, a scrawny, teenaged shepherd boy, to take down the mighty Goliath! In the passage from First Corinthians, God reveals how He delights in using people and things that we, in our human nature, would call unlikely, or even unqualified. God delights in these things because they give Him glory. Sometimes it takes us a while to see God's hand working, but when we do, we lift up our voices to glorify Him, saying, "Wow, Lord! It's amazing what You did in that situation!" After all, we were created for God's pleasure and to give Him glory (Revelation 4:11).

At first, I was apprehensive about Mr. Trump. I saw him as an arrogant, profane man during his campaign. He's been married three times. He was frequently swearing and insulting people. But then, Trump chose Mike Pence as his running mate for Vice President. Mr. Pence is known to be a godly man of integrity and character. Soon after Donald Trump was elected, I viewed him as Nebuchadnezzar and Mike Pence as Daniel. Throughout the campaign and within the last year, I have no doubt that God has used Mr. Pence to give Trump wisdom and teach him what God and His Word says about various subjects. But why Trump? Why did God give him the presidency?

First, I believe that Mr. Trump started with a vision. Proverbs 29:18 says, "Where there is no vision, the people perish..." Before Trump ran for President, I believe he saw where this country was at and where it was headed, and it wasn't good. So, he decided to step up. He did that by making himself available, by submitting himself as a candidate. He went out believing that he could make a difference in our great nation. It was a hard, long road for him when he refused to be a part of the Establishment.

The GOP, as a whole, was failing their constituents for far too long, America needed a president who would get back to work for the people, yesterday! And Trump was willing to be that president.

After making himself available, President Trump got busy. Being the clever entrepreneur that he is, I wouldn't doubt that he laid out plans for what he would do both during his candidacy and for if he was elected as President. As Christians, we understand what it means to be diligent in all that we do. Waiting on the Lord doesn't mean that we wait till He delivers. It means that we go about doing our Father's business. When David was told that he wasn't going to build the second Temple because of his sin, rather than making that an excuse to do nothing, he got the materials organized and ready for his son, Solomon, when he became king. Likewise, Trump got things in order.

Because of Donald Trump's vision for our country, his availability, and busyness, our Lord Jesus Christ committed, or appointed, him to the throne, as it were, over the United States of America. After his election, Trump brought the books out and planned what he was going to do for the first 100 days in office. As a businessman, Trump knew that it was wise to lay things out into decently and in order. Then, after the inauguration, President Trump got right to work, rather than celebrating right away. He started by making and signing executive orders to do away with some of the mess that the previous administration left behind.

As his first year office was continuing to unfold, people, minus the cynics and critics, witnessed Mr. Trump's devotion to our wonderful nation. He hasn't done everything right, but no one has or does. His tweets are sometimes undesirable, but other times it's refreshing to see him calling out folks who seek to ruin America. But he has done some favorable things for Christians.

One is him attempting to repeal the Johnson Amendment, which threatens the tax exempt status of churches should they engage in activity on behalf of or in opposition to any candidate for public office. There is a big lie out there saying that Christians have no business in getting involved in politics. One, the idea of separation of church and state means that the government cannot interfere with the affairs of a local church, since churches are to be run autonomously. Furthermore, this concept is not in our Constitution. It was mentioned in letter from Thomas Jefferson to a Baptist church. The violation of the separation of church and state can be illustrated by the account of King Saul and the prophet Samuel in 1 Samuel 13:8-14: "And he (Saul) tarried seven days, according to the set time that Samuel had appointed: but Samuel came not to Gilgal; and the people were scattered from him. And Saul said, Bring hither a burnt-offering to me, and peace-offerings. And he offered the burnt-offering. And it came to pass, that as soon as he had made an end of offering the burnt offering, behold, Samuel came; and Saul went out to meet him, that he might salute him. And Samuel said, what hast thou done? And Saul said, Because I saw that the people were scattered from me, and that thou camest not within the days appointed, and that the Philistines gathered themselves together at Michmash; Therefore, said I, The Philistines will come down now upon me to Gilgal, and I have not made supplication unto the LORD: I forced myself therefore, and offered a burnt-offering. And Samuel said to Saul, Thou hast done foolishly: thou hast not kept the commandment of the LORD thy God, which he commanded thee: for now would the LORD have established thy kingdom upon Israel for ever. But now thy kingdom shall not continue: the LORD hath sought him a man after his own heart, and the LORD hath commanded him to be captain over his people, because thou hast not kept that which the LORD commanded thee." From this passage, we can picture Saul as the "state" and the temple as the "church." The sacrifices in the temple were only allowed to be done by the priests. So, in that sense, Saul violated the separation of church and state. Secondly, God's people have always been involved in government. Moses had power under Pharaoh; Joseph was like the "right-hand man" of Pharaoh; Daniel was a statesman to Nebuchadnezzar, Belshazzar, Darius, and Cyrus. Paul was actually a missionary to kings. Acts 9:15 actually says, "But the Lord said unto him (Ananias), Go thy way: for he is a chosen vessel unto me, to bear my name before the Gentiles, and kings, and the children of Israel." Remember, God established the institution of government. So, it would be foolish to say that His people should have no part in government when God expects us to be.

When Trump first took office, he looked diligently and carefully concerning who he would choose for his Cabinet. This verse comes to mind: "Take away the wicked from before the king, and his throne shall be established in righteousness" (Proverbs 25:5). President Donald Trump sought for men and women that he believed were men and women of both integrity and character. He didn't make his decisions lightly. On top of their integrity and character, some members were actually Christians and people with a fighting spirit. These people are speaking up and standing for God. The media just can't help themselves, but to rail against the Trump administration. But Trump and his members just play them like a fiddle! Christians aren't always called to keep quiet. The Bible says that there is a time of war and a time of peace (Ecclesiastes 3:8). We are called soldiers. And these people, I believe, are good soldiers of Christ. We should no more seek to please man, but to please God as we are called and expected to.

One last thing I would like to recognize that Trump has done, was the moving of Israel's embassy back to Jerusalem. Jerusalem has always belonged to Israel. And we need to be a friend to Israel if we want to continue to receive God's blessings. God made this promise to Abraham: "And I will bless them that bless thee, and curse him that curseth thee" (Genesis 12:3). It should be noted here that there is no such thing as replacement theology. Meaning that the Church does not replace Israel. Please read the Book of Revelation and the Book of Daniel carefully to understand this truth.

Now with all that I said, I do not know if our President is truly saved. I hope he is. But regardless of what we think, we are all expected and commanded to pray for him, as we are to pray for everyone else. 1

Timothy 2:1-6 says, "I exhort therefore, that, first of all, supplications, prayers, intercessions, and giving of thanks, be made for all men; For kings, and for all that are in authority; that we may lead a quiet and peaceable life in all godliness and honesty. For this is good and acceptable in the sight of God our Saviour; Who will have all men to be saved, and to come unto the knowledge of the truth. For there is one God, and one mediator between God and

men, the man Christ Jesus; Who gave himself a ransom for all, to be testified in due time."

This passage indicates that everyone is a sinner in need of Christ, Who, died for all. That includes President Donald Trump. What Christian would think that anyone, including the President, should go to hell? If a professing Christian would place hope in that, then he should make sure that his own eternity is secure. The love of Christ is not in that person. 1 John 4:8 says that "He that loveth not (souls) knoweth not God; for God is love." If you don't know God, you're not saved. If you don't love souls, you're not saved. 2 Peter 3:9 says, "The Lord is not slack concerning his promise, as some men count slackness; but is longsuffering to us-ward, not willing that any should perish, but that all should come to repentance."

We know that Paul called himself the chief of sinners. But with human reasoning, we would say that Jezebel was far worse than Paul. She caused the children to fornicate, worship idols, and eat meat sacrificed to idols. However, God said this in Revelation 2:20-21: "Notwithstanding I have a few things against thee, because thou sufferest that woman Jezebel, which calleth herself a prophetess, to teach and to seduce my servants to commit fornication, and to eat things sacrificed unto idols. And I gave her space to repent of her fornication; and she repented not." Wow! Our Heavenly Father was so longsuffering with Jezebel, the most wicked person of her day, and desired for her to repent and get saved. If God could be so patient and so desirous for Jezebel's salvation, why couldn't He feel the same for our president? Or Obama or Hillary Clinton, for that matter? Our lack of prayers for lost souls shows our lack of love and care for them. O to be like that woman who pressed the unjust judge for justice until he finally turned and granted her request! We know that God is just. So how much more is He willing to answer our prayers for President Trump (or anyone)! Can you imagine what would happen in our country if the likes of Trump, Obama, and Hillary Clinton did get saved? Why, I imagine our country would be turned upside down and angels in heaven would be rejoicing!

Christian, it is my desire and prayer that you would join me in praying for President Trump's salvation and wisdom in ruling our country that we may live peaceably. Won't you join me?

Author of Refreshed In God's Word, Volume 1 and Cast Down Your Bucket article.

JOURNEY TO A WORLD CHAMPIONSHIP
Patricia M. Boord

I'm on the plane flying home after winning my very first world gold medal. The newness of being a world champion is still seemingly odd and unbelievable in an astonishing way.

Odd because I have desired to be a world champion since I competed in my first world bench press championship back in 2012. I never thought I'd achieve that level of performance. I'm still figuring out how to comfortably wear that title because I achieved it only by the grace of God. Unbelievable because of the obstacles that I needed to overcome along the way.

Wanting to capture my feelings as soon after my meet as possible, I began writing this article shortly after I got on the plane for home. But every time I tried to write and think about what I was feeling, my eyes continued to tear up. Occasionally a lone tear would escape from the corner of my eye and roll down my cheek. I've been doing that periodically since the gold medal was placed around my neck. They are tears of love -- both for the love I have for Jesus Christ, how He strengthened me to return to competing, and most importantly how He forgave me, a sinner. And, my patriotic love for the United States of America. Let me tell you how my journey began.

In April 2014, my son and I were enroute to my third World Masters Bench Press Championship in Newcastle upon Tyne, Northumbria, Great Britain. Getting ready to board the long leg of our flight, I reached down to pick-up my backpack and felt something snap in my lower back. Feeling instant pain, this wasn't good I thought.

During the flight, my back pain intensified and became increasing uncomfortable. Luckily, I brought along a couple of Lidocaine patches and decided to see if they would alleviate my pain. They did, but only a little.

The pain remained throughout the meet. Ice, Aleve, and the lidocaine patches diminished the pain slightly. I did fairly well at the meet and got two out of my three lifting attempts, but my back was not doing so well.

I took quite a few months off from training and my back pain subsided. In the fall, I was invited to be a member of the USA Powerlifting's National Team for 2015 which was slated to compete in Sweden. I returned to training and my back started to hurt again. By December the pain had intensified to the point where I was having difficulty getting into position to do a bench press. My coach was very concerned (and so was I) that I finally went to my orthopedic doctor for what I thought was going to be a cortisone injection. (Yes, I am a little stubborn by waiting so long.)

After seeing the x-rays from my back, my doctor immediately ordered an MRI and biopsy. The x-ray revealed a large white shadow on the left side of my lumbar region. Having suffered from septic arthritis in that area a couple of years earlier, he was extremely concerned that it had returned. After first setting the wheels in motion for some additional tests, my doctor contacted the infectious disease doctor who treated me for my earlier septic arthritis. The infectious disease doctor phoned later that day and insisted I immediately withdraw from the national team because of the potential seriousness of my back. So, I did.

I'm blessed to say that the biopsy, blood cultures, and other tests were all negative. But I still had a large white shadow on my x-ray and my back was extremely painful. I was referred to the University of Virginia (UVA) for further consultation. UVA did their own x-rays and additional MRIs. After consulting with other experts, they believed the best thing to do was wait. They didn't know what was wrong with my back. I didn't have a fever or any of the other symptoms associated with septic arthritis and both the biopsy and lab cultures were negative, so they believed that it was safe to wait. While I waited I had a monthly MRI over the course of several months to monitor any changes.

By July of 2015, UVA determined that I had an unusually herniated disk that popped out to the side because of the scoliosis in my lumbar back region. They were unable to see the herniated disk earlier because it had been extremely inflamed – hence the white shadow. Not lifting and resting my back enabled my body to fight off the inflammation. Still it remained painful and very tender to touch. They weren't keen on doing surgery and wanted to wait to see if I healed further with more rest.

After meeting with UVA in July, I rescheduled my right knee replacement for the following September. I was having so much back pain that my original June knee surgery had been postponed. I was to return to UVA about six weeks after my knee surgery to discuss possible back surgery.

The knee surgery went off without a hitch, except for some long standing post-op nausea, and I recovered quite quickly. I returned to UVA to see what the next step was going to be for my back. And guess what, my back no longer hurt!!! Thank you, Father!! The doctor poked and prodded but there was not pain. Nothing. I was released with the caveat, "Come back if the pain returns." I am blessed to say that it has been two years since that last appointment.

I was free to return to training, but I needed to modify my benching technique to make sure that my lower back remained in constant contact with the bench when I lifted. Otherwise, the pain would most likely return, and my competition days would be over.

Resuming training after a long hiatus was like starting all over again. I had to do that quite a few times since I began lifting to improve my health. I probably started over about seven times in the nine years I had been lifting. There were a lot of reasons for my training breaks: other surgeries, serious lung infections, a hiking fall, etc. But starting over again began to take a toll on me.

By January of 2016, I was beat down by that point and didn't know how many more times I could start over. Or, if I had any more "start overs" left in me. I cried out to God and literally cried my eyes out. God let me wallow in my own pity party for about two weeks. It was while I was at the gym when the Holy Spirit spoke to my heart. In the midst of struggling to lift a weight, the Holy Spirit told me that I would start over as many times as He needed me to. But, that He would be with me each time I did. Reassured that I wasn't alone, I'll do as you ask Father. I continued my training.

It was hard regaining my strength, but I knew that I wasn't alone. Little did I know how that moment of surrendering to God's will would continue to permeate my life during the next fifteen months.

Over two years had lapsed since I last competed. But I returned to the platform in March of 2016. It was a local meet in which I needed to compete, so I could qualify for the 2016 USA Powerlifting's Bench Press National Championship. The national championship is the gateway to international competitions. I did well at that meet and set my training sights on the national championship six months away.

Let me interrupt my story for a moment and tell you a little about myself. Competing is one of the ways in which I share my faith. I have a what I call *My Cross Project.* In November of 2014 I began carrying in my pocket, a small olive wood cross. The Holy Spirit asked me to carry that cross and share it with whomever He placed in my path. So, I did. He is so beautifully faithful with this project. When I first began, God knew that I was very nervous about walking up to a stranger and sharing a cross with them. At first, I only carried one cross in my pocket. Then the Holy Spirit suggested that I carry two crosses...then three. Well, folks I now carry a pocket full of them and have extras in my purse, my gym bag, and my truck. This project has opened many beautiful doors for me to pray, encourage, and comfort many of my fellow competitors, their families, and the total strangers I meet every day.

Arriving for the national championship in September 2016, I was two pounds underweight in the division I had entered. It was perfect. I was continually praying and asking God to guide my eating so that I could make weight. I always get stressed about making weight, but this time my prayer changed spontaneously about two weeks before the meet. God knew where my heart lay in relation to my weight. But I began surrendering by praying, "Thy will be done."

While waiting for the meet to begin, I carefully monitored my caloric and water intakes. But I found myself the day before weigh-ins, two pounds over the weight limit. At national level competitions, an athlete can change their weight class during weigh-ins. But this can't be done at international competitions. If you're overweight during an international meet, you go home without competing.

I got up extra early the morning of my competition and went to weigh myself on the "official" scale. Can you believe it. I wasn't two pounds overweight. I was two kilos over!! That's 4 pounds and 13 ounces over. But this time I didn't panic. Oh well, I thought. I'll compete at whatever weight God had chosen for me.

Returning to my room I took a shower and relaxed a little before it was time to get officially weighed. I had about forty minutes to wait. As I relaxed, I prayed and rested in the Lord's presence. I told myself that there was no way I could lose over four pounds in forty minutes. But as soon as that thought entered my mind, I immediately reminded myself that my God was bigger than that. I would compete at whatever weight He wanted me to. It was His will that I would follow.

I took the elevator down to weigh-ins and patiently waited my turn. I was comforted in knowing that God was with me. When it was my turn, I told the judge that I might need to move up a weight class. OK, she said. "Let's see what you weigh." My friends, I couldn't believe my eyes when I saw my weight displayed on the scale. I was 2.2 kilos *under* the weight limit!!! I was stunned. God had fulfilled my desire. I didn't stop to analyze what happened or determine if I read the scale incorrectly earlier that morning. It was irrelevant because God had chosen my weight and that was all that mattered. I did well at the meet and earned a spot on the 2017 USA Powerlifting National Team. I would complete at the next World Masters Classic Bench Press Championship in Texas in April 2017.

I must confess to you now that in the following January (2017), I had willfully done something against God's Word. I knew it was wrong, yet I did it. The type of sin that I committed is irrelevant. What's important is that I knew it was wrong, yet the weakness of my human soul won out over my faith. My friends, I wish that I could say that I immediately felt bad for what I did, but I didn't. That shocked me. It still does. I'm a very heartful person and always strive to do the best I can, and I quickly feel bad if I ever offend anyone. Yet, I willfully offended God. What had I done???

After a couple of days, I slowly began to realize the magnitude of my sinfulness. How could I have done that to my Lord? Rightfully so, God had turned Himself away from me because of my actions. Up until my sinning, the Holy Spirit and I were closely connected to each other. I felt Him always. He brought so much joy to my heart. Now, I felt completely alone, and it was my fault. I was empty.

On my knees, I earnestly prayed for forgiveness and cried rivers of tears. All the while knowing that He forgave me, yet still feeling empty. I'm usually a very upbeat and joyful person. But during that time of emptiness, it was very difficult for me share my joy with others. I'm the happy lady at the gym who is always encouraging others. It was hard for me to continue that behavior. That emptiness lasted for three months. Then it was Easter.

My flight to the 2017 World Masters Classic Bench Press Championship left early Easter morning. I felt lighthearted as I walked through the airport. After proceeding through security, I stopped at the nearest shop to buy a couple of liters of water. While there, I began chatting with the cashier. Being the only one in the store, she asked if I was a Christian and if I would pray with her that Easter morning. After praying, I gave her one of my crosses. I'll never forget her. She was about 5'6" tall with long straight black hair. Streaks of gray ran through the full length of her hair and found their way through a rubber band with which she secured it. She wore no make-up and looked like she had a hard life. Upon receiving the cross, she began weeping and told me how much it meant to her. She then took a full-sized piece of printer paper and wrapped it around the cross. Finally, she tucked the wrapped cross in her bra. She was quite a buxom lady and that printer paper with its sharp corners could not have felt comfortable. But that's where she placed it.

I arrived in Texas safely and began to connect with other USA competitors. I wasn't there long before I found myself praying and crying with a woman whose husband had cancer. Then I was praying with her husband who was one of the meet's officials. I continued to share crosses and pray with many of the USA lifters. At one point, several of us sat in the back of the lifting venue and had our own prayer session.

The next afternoon, my coach and I went to a local restaurant to have some lunch. While there, I met a young mom from the local area with the most adorable little boy. She came and sat near our table and asked if we were in town for the world powerlifting meet. We were and that opened an extended conversation with her. She was such a beautiful soul who was also hurting. Wanting to improve her health, she felt overwhelmed by everything that was wrong with her. We chatted for a while and after giving her a cross, we prayed right there in the restaurant.

I continued to share crosses and prayed with many competitors. In fact, my coach (who is a strong Christian), commented that if I didn't lift well the next morning, my meet would have been very successful because of my ministering. It wasn't my lifting that was of paramount important, sharing my faith and the love of Jesus Christ was my priority. I felt full of wonder as the Lord's presence had returned to my heart.

Before I knew it, the time had come for me to compete. My lifting went very well, and I made all three of my lifts. I was the world champion!!! Standing on the podium while our national anthem played was something that I don't think I'll ever forget. Tears freely rolled down my cheeks. In fact, I don't have any pictures of me smiling while I'm holding our flag. Yes, I had finally won a world championship.

Winning that gold medal pales in comparison to my Lord's grace and forgiveness. I sinned against Him and didn't deserve this accomplishment. And I still don't deserve His blessings. But reflecting back upon all that had transpired, my eyes have been opened to how I began to abide in Him. It was if I was re-born that Easter morning. I am a new creature in Christ. I felt the Holy Spirit increase His presence in me as I ministered to those around me. That's why I still well up with tears when I think back to that meet. Yes, winning the championship was a great accomplishment, but regaining my relationship with my Lord and Savior Jesus Christ is much, much more valuable. I cry for winning that medal and for winning back my soul. Thank you, Father. I am nothing without you and owe all that I am to you. Amen.

BABY BOOMER REPORT CARDS NOW AVAILABLE
Angelo Paul Ramunni

I was born in 1948 and thereby became an early member of the Baby Boomer generation whose members were born between the years of 1946 and 1964.

We were born during a time when people were looking to enjoy life after experiencing the Great Depression and World War II. The United States was redirecting its enormous productive energies toward developing consumer and industrial goods. Our parents wanted us to have all the good things they never had when they grew up. Consequentially, many of us Boomers stepped into a time when much opportunity and wealth were being created and therefore, we were in the best position for accomplishing great things, perhaps more than any other generation before us.

When many of us started to become of age in the 1960's, we were faced with making a choice between living our lives according to the beliefs and moral codes of our parents, or to develop our own set of values. Many of my peers were opting for living life their own way. They chose to make their own choices according to their own desires and needs at the time. I remember back in 1969 when Woodstock occurred and over four hundred thousand young people gathered on a farm in upstate New York and displayed to the world what our generation believed in and how we wanted to live. Much to the consternation of older generations, people just could not believe how fast we were abandoning the learned wisdom and ways of the past and exchanging them for unproven and radical ways of living.

Our Boomer generation was seen as indulging itself in whatever it wanted. The sexual revolution of the 60's turned sex into a recreational activity. Drugs and alcohol were being consumed at alarming rates. No-fault divorce became a legal reality along with the most significant change of all, on-demand abortion. Meanwhile, manufacturers were pumping out more and more consumer goods that people wanted. In order to afford these things, people needed more money. So, personal credit became available principally in the form of credit cards. For the first time in all of human history, people no longer had to work first, save the money, and then buy the things they wanted. Instead they now could borrow against their future earnings in order to make the purchases they wanted now. Bankruptcy laws were also being modified to help people caught up in overspending.

Another most interesting development was the need to adjust how God would look upon all of these changes. Many of us Boomers were raised in the Judeo-Christian faith system. Whether Catholic, Protestant or Jewish, we were taught that there was a God. It soon became obvious that the direction our generation was heading in was not in sync with Biblical scripture. To deal with that, many of us simply stopped going to church. But true to our consumerist society, other forms of

Christianity began to pop up in order make it easier for folks to follow Jesus and still have all of the aforementioned liberties. In essence, we no longer needed to become born again but rather Christ would be born again for each of us. We could customize and remake Him into a god that we could live with… a more "user friendly Jesus." In essence we changed places with Him. We made our wants and desires all important and Christ was now available to help us acquire these things.

Today, as our generation starts entering our retirement years, something else has developed that threatens the very core of our society. We always had the ability to work out our differences concerning how we govern and live with one another. Compromise was the course of action most frequently taken when there were disagreements. It seems that option no longer is available. Our country is divided in many ways over many issues. The division lies along political party lines, principally liberals versus conservatives. It has progressed to the point where rational discussion cannot be had without strong negative feelings developing.

I remember when my office, where I teach at a local university, was adjacent to a world history teacher's office. We would talk about how fewer and fewer people agree on anything that comes up in life. He would refer me back to the years just before the Civil War. He said that if you read the newspaper clippings of that time period, you would find much of the same vitriol and anger that we have today. He also told me that since we disagree on the needed solutions, out of frustration, people will typically begin to hate those who oppose them. Once that hatred spreads into the general public, finding common sense solutions becomes virtually impossible. It seems that this is where we are today. How can we live together and move forward given these circumstances?

We need to change our focus.

Since we Boomers began coming of age in the '60's, our focus has mainly been on ourselves and our wants. Interestingly, at that time researchers hired by Burger King to develop a more effective sales slogan, came up with *"Have it Your Way."* That accurately described our generation.

Since then the focus has indeed been on us having things our way. Prior to our generation's arrival on the scene, there was a different focus. God played more of a major role in society. Our country was seen as being Christian based. People seemed to care more for one another's welfare. I believe it was easier to settle disagreements back then because our common spiritual heritage was more generally accepted.

We all know that over the last 60 + years, God has slowly been removed from virtually every area of our public lives. He is no longer in our educational system, the mainstream media, our government, and most certainly is absent from the entire entertainment industry. The vast majority of organized sporting events, even down to grammar school levels, business transactions and most other societal activities are performed without any reference to God. As a result, we have been losing that all important spiritual link with God and one another.

About five years ago, at age sixty-five, I had a major heart attack. I managed to survive and was lucky enough not to have any lasting ill effects. But it was my wake-up call. I came to realize that most of my life was behind me at that point. I could actually look back over my years and see key actions I had taken, both good and bad. It was like watching a movie based on my life. I was unhappy with some of what I saw and realized suddenly that I was looking at my "life's report card."

Many of my friends have already retired from work and made up their "bucket lists" of things they still want to do. And that is fine. But for me, as I look back, I see something different. My bucket list has become a list of the things God still wants me to accomplish in the time I have left.

Let me explain.... this is very important.

It was early 1990 when I found a little book entitled "In His Steps" by Charles Sheldon. It asked that famous question "What Would Jesus Do?" It really had an impact on me. It changed my thinking and my actions, so I would be more in line with how Christ Himself would live my life. That change has not been easy to make. In the process, I have come to see that Jesus Christ is real as He has personally intervened many times in my life.

But what if we all started to think that way today? What would Jesus say and do if He was here again like He was some two thousand years ago? How would He approach the hatred issue that we have for one another created by our differing political beliefs?

If we go back into the gospels, nowhere do you see Christ engaging in the politics of His day. It is really amazing. The Romans were a constant threat to the Jews. They were harassing and killing them on a daily basis. But He said and did nothing to change that. Jesus kept His message simple. He told us to love God and one another. Regardless of what you may think about Christ, whether He was God or not, His philosophy of loving others cannot be improved upon. And where are we today in relation to that philosophy? In fact, we are on the opposite side of it. Our hatred for one another keeps us in direct opposition to Christ.

Christ engages each of us on a personal basis in order to get us to take a look at the current status of our report card. *You do not have to wait until judgment day to find out what's on your report card. You can see it now <u>while you still have time to improve it.</u>* Report cards come out as soon as we reach that age where more time is behind us than is still in front of us. Take a good look at your report card. Were you correct in your choice of values and beliefs? How many people in need did you help? Has your life truly worked out for you?

Consider the stories in the NEWS these days. If the beliefs and actions we embraced in the past were correct, wouldn't today's NEWS stories be more positive? We have to be very honest with ourselves. By refocusing our view of how we handled events in our past, we may be able to change our thoughts and actions toward people presently in our lives and remove some of the hatred that exists.

Christ began His public ministry by telling people to repent. It was the most important message for the people of that day, as it is for us. We need to change our way of thinking about life and other people. In turn that will help us change our actions. Why is this so absolutely important? Because we are coming to that point in life when we will find out what is on the other side. We will see the life that is to follow this one, and we will meet the gatekeeper to that life.

There is only one thing left in life that has a 100% chance of occurring. We will all die.... even Jesus had to die. We are told there will then be a judgment for each and every person. I would expect that our personal report cards will weigh heavily in God's decision as to where we will spend eternity.

Take a look at how Christ outlines in detail the judgment day and how it will be conducted:

"When the Son of Man comes in his glory, and all the angels with him, then he will sit on his glorious throne. Before him will be gathered all the nations, and he will separate people one from another as a shepherd separates the sheep from the goats. And he will place the sheep on his right, but the goats on the left. Then the King will say to those on his right, 'Come, you who are blessed by my Father, inherit the kingdom prepared for you from the foundation of the world. For I was hungry, and you gave me food, I was thirsty, and you gave me drink, I was a stranger and you welcomed me, I was naked, and you clothed me, I was sick, and you visited me, I was in prison and you came to me.' Then the righteous will answer him, saying, 'Lord, when did we see you hungry and feed you, or thirsty and give you drink? And when did we see you a stranger and welcome you, or naked and clothe you? And when did we see you sick or in prison and visit you?' And the King will answer them, 'Truly, I say to you, as you did it to one of the least of these my brothers, you did it to me.'

"Then he will say to those on his left, 'Depart from me, you cursed, into the eternal fire prepared for the devil and his angels. For I was hungry, and you gave me no food, I was thirsty, and you gave me no drink, I was a stranger and you did not welcome me, naked and you did not clothe me, sick and in prison and you did not visit me.' Then they also will answer, saying, 'Lord, when did we see you hungry or thirsty or a stranger or naked or sick or in prison, and did not minister to you?' Then he will answer them, saying, 'Truly, I say to you, as you did not do it to one of the least of these, you did not do it to me.' And these will go away into eternal punishment, but the righteous into eternal life." Matthew 25:31-46

So, let's review all of this...

-We know that there will be a "final exam" given on judgment day.

-We have access now to the correct answers to the exam as noted in the above Scripture.

-We know how it will be graded, and who will be doing the grading.

-And amazingly, we are being given extra time now to improve our current report card results in order to receive full credit.

-This is the best opportunity we will ever receive in our entire lives!

Review you report card... change your focus... there still is time. Do it quickly and watch what God will do.

Angelo Paul Ramunni
2018

A GUIDE TO FINDING ONE'S PATH
Selina Maxwell

Do you ever give serious consideration as to how much we are a part of Mother Nature and how we both operate in similar patterns?

Mother Nature has her seasons of growth and dormancy with occasional unexpected storms and other events that have their own time table and cause and effect. Earthquakes, volcanoes, tsunamis, hurricanes, tornadoes, and fires make the news to inform us as to other world events and their results on humanity. Our awareness is brought to the forefront of those events.

We too go through patterns of growth, dormancy, perhaps even failure, illness, or ruptured relationships or loss of a loved one.

Life is not a constant state of being. It ebbs and flows, and our life storms can present us with not only the unexpected but can stretch us beyond what we thought were our capabilities or capacities to function or carry on.

Shocks in whatever manner they occur can leave us trapped in our own woefulness and self-pity. Grieving and experiencing a sense of loss is natural. What is not natural is to stay concretized in that place of feeling hurt or in pain constantly wondering, "Why did that happen to me?" or wishing to relive the past repeatedly stalemating ourselves from moving forward to the next level or into a new direction. That is not living. It is subjugation by one's own hand. Memories and one's life experiences are assembled or integrated into our emotional, mental and physical selves. We do have to heal to a certain level to move forward. We also have to DECIDE To HEAL.

In the darkest moments of one's life, one is never truly alone. God is always close at hand observing our efforts, activities and interactions with others in whatever capacity they may be, personal, family or professional.

For those individuals who are unsure of God's Presence in their lives, I would say "Yes, it is hard to believe in the unseen, but yes, the unseen exists all around us." We live in an energy world. It exists all around us and we take it for granted when we turn on our lights, TV, radio, computer and cells phones. Energy and frequencies inundate us. We cannot see them, but we know they are there.

God Energy is the highest energy available to us. It is an intangible, yet it exists. God and His Power surround and pervade us all. What do we do to tap into it? How do we connect with it on a regular basis? The first step is prayer. Not just when we are in trouble and need His Help. Daily prayer is fine tuning the connection to God. It is like muscle building or a strengthening process. We are what we eat, and we are what we feed our spiritual selves. Time in prayer helps to ground us and gain a sense of clarity and peace.

One cannot force this desire for prayer on others, even one's own children will have to acknowledge its value in their lives in their own time. We can lead our children in prayer at a young age and through Sunday school, however like everything else the final choices in life are theirs. Circumstances, work, relationships require time, effort and navigation through life. They may act as a deterrent to some extent and cause one to veer off course from one's spiritual journey.

It is our desire to seek that which is outside of ourselves, to turn our faces to God and build the tie that binds. We will be richer for it. No other riches in life can compare. I cannot think of one. God waits for us to seek Him on our own volition. It is our own desire to do this that turns the ignition on. We awake or act at different times and in different communication styles in which the tie is strengthened – Father-Child bonding at its highest.

Parents realize that they cannot teach their children everything about life and decision making. Sometimes veering off course is the lesson a child needs to understand what serves him or her well and what does not. Letting children go can be very difficult, but it is their need for discovery about the essentials and fundamentals of life that are their lessons to be learned. God is incredibly patient with us as we do the same exploration and veer off course, no matter what our age. The more stumbling blocks that appear, perhaps the more attention we should be paying to Him and the choices we are making.

Even Mother Nature is governed by an unseen hand. Who regulates her knowing of seasonal function, bird migration, animal procreation, and even the insect world. Plants, flowers and trees all have a pattern of existence.

We view and accept these things on a regular basis, as they are part of our ecology. We accept them without reservation. We watch our gardens grow and tend to them to promote more growth. We anticipate the results of future harvests and our rewards therein. This orchestration of Mother Nature follows a pattern. She is governed by a Higher Power who is not seen or heard but it is there operating on frequencies and patterns.

We too are governed by a Higher Power that surrounds the environment we live in. We are enmeshed in it. How does a mother sense intuitively what is wrong with her child or what it needs for comfort? How do healthy close relationships grow and help one another thrive? This unseen energy comes from the heart. It is called Love. Love is what we should consider cultivating in ourselves to the best of our ability. In healthy sustenance of our bodies, minds and souls, we become more finely attuned and open to God's Grace. We will have ears to hear and hearts to follow.

Matthew 6:33

"But seek first the Kingdom of God, and his righteousness; and all these things shall be added unto you."

Romans 12:2

"And be not conformed to this world: but be ye transformed by the renewing of your mind, that ye may prove what is that good, and acceptable, and perfect, will of God."

1 Corinthians 3:16

"Know ye not that ye are the temple of God, and that the Spirit of God dwelleth in you?"

Genesis 1:27

"So, God created man in his own image , in the image of God, He created him; male and female he created them."

Divine creation is in our pattern of existence. It is how we came to be. It is up to us to keep our temple bodies clean and nurtured to allow the Glory of God to further manifest in our bodies and into our lives. We would not consider for a moment deliberately polluting the food we put into our bodies and expect our bodies to thrive. In cleansing our bodies and focus on daily prayer we become stronger, more clear and finely attuned to the Lord who made us.

Daily prayer and giving thanks in our prayers. Yes, prayer is a choice each individual has to make. Intermittent prayer in a time of need only is akin to casual exercise. What are the long term benefits? Giving thanks on a daily basis to God is honoring His Presence in one's life. Yes, it is all about choice for each of us. We can veer off the path, but we can also choose to get back on that path. No-one else can do it for you.

Prayer is a soulful communication with God. It is not a mechanical process. Prayer carries with it deep feeling, emotion, sincerity and reverence. Daily incorporation of prayer into one's life nurtures the soul in unseen ways. It is an intangible vehicle that strengthens our ties to our spiritual being and to our God.

Life makes many demands on our time. We take on many responsibilities that can diffuse spiritual grounding. With spiritual grounding there is a centeredness, peace and awareness that takes hold and germinates through our being. It adds strength to our being and clarity into our lives. There is no greater value system that gives us Divine Protection and Guidance. None.

People are drawn to develop their own individual communication channels from selections in the Bible. Some personal preferences from the King James Version of the Bible are:

Psalm 23

Psalm 27

Psalm 70

Psalm 91

Psalm 117

Matthew – Chapter 7 – Verses 7 & 8

7. "Ask and it shall be given you; seek and ye shall find; knock and it shall be opened unto you."

8. "For everyone that asketh receiveth; and he that seeketh findeth; and to him that knocketh, it shall be opened."

The Lord's Prayer is said in reverence prior to the above.

There is a fine example of unseen power that you may have read before. It is a quote from the Scottish Himalayan Expedition by W.H. Murray:

"Until one is committed there is hesitancy, the chance to draw back, always ineffectiveness. Concerning all acts of initiative or creation, there is one elementary truth... that the moment one definitely commits oneself, then Providence moves, too. All sorts of things occur to help one that would otherwise never have occurred. A whole stream of events issues from the decision, raising in one's favor all manner of incidents and meetings and material assistance which no man would have believed would have come his way.

Whatever you think you can do or believe you can do, begin it. Action has magic, grace, and power in it."

W. H. Murray – Quotable Quote

We are not alone. There is abundance in the universe. It is God's abundance. People see and hear of miracles all the time. It is the work of God's Divine Hand and His fleet of angels who work among us.

We are cared for, protected and loved by the unseen Hand of God. His energy is felt even though His Presence may be physically unseen. He gently surrounds us in ways that cannot be adequately defined in this physical world. The power of belief and prayer draws us closer to Him and strengthens the ties and the Glory of God in our lives.

Seek the Kingdom of God. Why?

Matthew 6:33 But seek ye first the Kingdom of God, and his righteousness; and all these things shall be added unto you.

Romans 10:13 For "everyone who calls on the name of the Lord will be saved."

Be Blessed,
Love to All
Selina Maxwell
www.selinamaxwell.com

UNITY
Apostle Terri Diggs

Deeply seated in our commandment to Love is a distinctness of a non-violent nature, yet we are moved by that same compassion which causes us to move past ourselves to meet the needs of others, even, until the point death.

It is with this same compassion I speak to you this day:
"I am going to stand up in the midst of persecutions, accusations, religious spirits, and even death, armed with truth."

If I had a choice of where I would take my stand, it would be in the midst of Acts 15: before the Sanhedrin in Jerusalem with: The Apostle's Peter, Paul, and Barnabas, I would bring them on a journey back to Genesis. All with an understanding, that Jesus with His blood would wipe the slate clean; because of Him "old things have passed away and all things have become new", we have an opportunity to choose for ourselves.

We would find ourselves in the midst of that same choice between the trees in which Adam and Eve chose: the tree of the knowledge of good and evil, and the tree of Life. I would proceed to display the truth about this tree in which we have lived. This tree must have good, and it must have evil, and because Eve chose this tree and ultimately caused the fall of mankind: male and female she was considered evil, and Adam was considered good.

We have lived in a society where everything has been divided into these two categories from television to real life. If we are to understand fully, then we must understand this is the root of racisms of all kind: Jews and Gentiles, Blacks and Whites, Yellows and Reds. Even within one's own race it is broken down to the lights and the darks, the rich and the poor until it ultimately comes back to male and female. Yes, back to Genesis,

We have come back to this place to make a choice. We must choose, for in not choosing we have chosen. So, we must choose between the tree of the knowledge of good and evil and the tree of Life. Who is this tree of Life? His name is Jesus. In John 14:6 Jesus declares He is the way the truth and the Life, and in choosing Him it is unmistakably your choice; no one can choose for you. For His path is a single file. Because strait is the gate, and narrow is the way, which leadeth unto life, and few there be that find it. (Matthew 7:14)

Ahh! He didn't say that someone couldn't show you the way. If you have chosen Life, the definition for that is God's Word written upon the tables of your heart. Be it male or female, God writes His law, and His Commandments on your heart.

The first of which states: "Thou shalt have no other gods before Me." Because of this law we have come down through history living a lie.

(Exodus 20:3)

For too long we have lived within the confines of the tree of knowledge of good and evil, thus nullifying the death, burial and resurrection of Life Himself (Jesus Christ). Mesmerized by the effects of this tree we have placed man in the position of God. As a result, we have continually sinned against Almighty God. We have offended our God, in that we laid aside His Love for us.

The Apostle that I am, would ask the question: *Thou shalt have no other god before Me (God): does this apply to Women?* Even amid tradition, and strong opposition, there could be no other answer but "YES."

Moreover, I would declare that the same defense they agreed on against the yoke of tradition is the same defense that justifies women; for the Holy Spirit bears witness to them this day and forevermore. It is the evidence of speaking in tongues and prophecy that brings the seal of Life, God's Word, on the inside.

Acts 15:6-12

6) And the apostles and elders came together for to consider of this matter.

7) And when there had been much disputing, Peter rose up, and said unto them, 'Men and brethren, ye know how that a good while ago God made choice among us, that the Gentiles by my mouth should hear the word of the gospel and believe.

8) And God, which knoweth the hearts, bare them witness, giving them the Holy Ghost, even as he did unto us;

9) And put no difference between us and them, purifying their hearts by faith.

10) Now therefore why tempt ye God, to put a yoke upon the neck of the disciples, which neither our fathers nor we were able to bear?

11) But we believe that through the grace of the Lord Jesus Christ we shall be saved, even as they.'

12) Then all the multitude kept silence, and gave audience to Barnabas and Paul, declaring what miracles and wonders God had wrought among the Gentiles by them.

I would go on and give an illustration showing what we as mankind are as images of God:

Male	Plus	Female		Man	Image of God
Soul (mind)	+	Soul (mind)	=		Father
body		body			Son
spirit		spirit			Holy Spirit
3	Cross	3		6	3

God is Love. God Himself being Love gives us the recipe for love: if you follow His Commandment you love yourself, and if you love yourself you love God and if you love God you will love mankind. Herein is Love, because you are the image of God, keeping His Commandments, loving God and loving mankind, both with Spirit (spirit) mind (soul) and body.

I would declare to you today the true Declaration of Independence is written upon the tables of the heart.

It is evident by Acts 5 with Ananias and Sapphira how we will be judged for ourselves, that's right One on one with God.

The wedding vows in particular are most offensive to God; the traditional marriage vows cause a partition between God and women. You see, no longer can good approach God; there is no more option for good and evil. Only Life can approach God.

This is not merely a quest for freedom for women, but for mankind: male and female.

Alas, we would have to step into the time of Isaiah to gather the recipe for unity, "where there is unity God commands the Blessing of life for evermore", Psalms 133.

Isaiah declares that:

4) Every valley shall be exalted, and every mountain and hill shall be made low: and the crooked shall be made straight, and the rough places plain:

5) And the glory of the LORD shall be revealed, and all flesh shall see *it* together: for the mouth of the LORD hath spoken *it*.

Isaiah 40:4,5

It is unity that opens the door to the Promise Land. Together, through the Holy Spirit, we can partake of every promise that God has given us. Male cannot be man without female, nor can female be man without male.

This is Promise Land Ministries,
Apostle Terri Diggs
Under the reigns of the Holy Ghost

WHAT ARE MY OPTIONS?
by
Dr. Steven George Coy

Newspaper columnist William Safire once wrote a pre-election column that posed this question: "What do you do when a candidate of your choice takes a position you don't like, or when the candidate you oppose takes a stand that you admire?"

Safire suggested there were three options of response: 1) Switch candidates 2) Stay with your candidate and wear a button that says, "Nobody's perfect" or 3) Be like the proverbial old woman who says, "I never vote. It only encourages them." She chose to stay passive, not choose, do nothing. The question by Safire also has some interesting spiritual applications concerning personal choice.

The Apostle Peter quoted the prophet Isaiah and the Psalmist when he wrote the following passage, "Therefore, it is also contained in the Scripture, 'Behold, I lay in Zion a chief cornerstone, elect, precious, and he who believes on Him will by no means be put to shame.' Therefore, to you who believe, He is precious; but to those who are disobedient, 'The Stone which the builders rejected has become the chief cornerstone, ' and 'A stone of stumbling and rock of offense.' They stumble, being disobedient to the word, to which they also were appointed." (1 Peter 2:6-8)

This passage of Scripture implies that the words of Christ will not always be popular to His followers nor to the casual listener. His words of truth will cause some to stumble and some to take offense. The result will be that many followers will switch candidates or find someone else to follow--someone who speaks more agreeable words, or who represents a less rigid standard.

The Apostle Paul also referred to Christ as a stumbling stone. He was speaking to Jews who were trying to earn their righteousness (right standing before God) by works and through good deeds. Because Christ represented righteousness available by faith and faith alone, they did not like his teaching nor what He represented-- righteousness by grace to anyone who would believe on Him. Thus, the Jews stumbled at the Rock of offense, "Because they did not seek it (righteousness) by faith, but as it were, by the works of the law. For they stumbled at that stumbling stone (Christ)." (Romans 9:32)

Peter was once faced with the question, WHAT ARE MY OPTIONS? Jesus had just given a teaching that his followers found difficult to swallow and "many went back and walked with Him no more." He turned to Peter and asked, "Do you also want to go away?" Peter considered the question, considered the options, and answered, "Lord, to whom shall we go? You have the words of eternal life." Peter chose to believe the words of the Lord. (John 6:66-68)

How about you? Are you a loyal, dedicated follower who heeds the words of the Master, no matter how they may go against your old ways of thinking or current patterns of behavior? Does your heart sing continually, "I have decided to follow Jesus, no turning back, no turning back." Or are you one who just may decide to follow someone or something else when things don't go your way? Perhaps you are one who knows to believe in Jesus Christ but who actually believes in Jesus Plus-- Jesus plus psychology, Jesus plus philosophy, Jesus plus personal opinion, or Jesus plus anything contrary to the teachings of his Word...

WHAT ARE MY OPTIONS? Every living soul must ask this question and choose. One must choose to allow Christ to be the guiding Light and Lord of life, or to be a stumbling Stone and Rock of offense. Those are the options. We either believe absolutely what He has said and Who He claims to be, or we choose something or someone else--we stumble over his claims, his words, his Self. The result of the choice is either to stumble because of disobedience to his words (verse 8) or be honored because we have found Him and his words both worthy and precious (verse 7).

May God's grace abound toward you from this day forward as you compare Christ with any other so-called hope the world may offer. May you not stumble at this Stone, may you not be offended by this Rock. May you choose the Truth, "So that...with hearts sincere and certain and unsullied--you may approach the day of

Christ, not stumbling nor causing others to stumble."
(Philippians 1:10)

In this choice, one cannot, as the old woman did, stay passive, not choose, or do nothing. To not make a decisive choice has eternal consequences--judgment. To make a decisive choice for Christ also has consequences-- the gift of eternal life, "...that whoever believes in Him should not perish but have everlasting life." (John 3:16)

One must consider carefully and eternally the awesome question, "WHAT ARE MY OPTIONS?"

* * * * *

For more published works by Dr. Coy, go to www.TheChristianOutdoorsman.com or www.CMHbook.com. To view his video productions, go to the White Eagle Exploits channel at www.YouTube.com.

PEACE IN THE MIDST OF PAIN
Christine Chang

"And the peace of God, which transcends all understanding, will guard your hearts and your minds in Christ Jesus."

—Philippians 4:7 (NIV)

He was a bundle of chaos and energy. We would call him Stitch, the little blue alien from the Disney movie, a character whose sole purpose in life was to wreak havoc on the world around him. Mama would laugh when there was nothing else she could do. "Such is life with Jonathan," she would say. "And the chaos continues!"

When the flecks and speckles appeared like paint splatters on his baby chest, Jonathan didn't slow his pace. Not even the fever and or brief bouts of fatigue could keep him down for long. But when the symptoms didn't subside, my parents grew more and more concerned.

The doctor's diagnosis—leukemia—affected the rest of us more than it did the two-year-old tyke.

In my memory, that moment is frozen in time. My mother faced me with wide, bloodshot eyes.

"Jonathan has cancer."

My blood ran cold.

Most of what she said after that is a blur. General impressions remain, but the details are surrounded by a haze. There were things that had to be done—so much that needed to be put in order. Mom needed help packing. She needed clothes for herself and Jonathan. She needed me to find Jonathan's favorite movie. She needed to go with him to the hospital in the big city.

Still, I was trapped in that moment of revelation.

Jonathan had cancer.

My brother. My baby brother. The little one, the crazy one, the one who never slowed down.

Cancer.

"Mom?" I asked.

She didn't slow her packing. "Yes, honey?"

"Is Jonathan going to die?"

She stopped then. When she looked at me, her eyes held an unfathomable pain, too much for a child my age to understand.

"I don't know, sweetie," she murmured. "Not even the doctors can be sure yet. Only God knows."

Which was scarier: my brother's illness, or the fact that my mother—my strong, wise, all-knowing mommy— didn't know what would happen to him?

With that, I broke down. Mom took me, sobbing, into her arms. The warmth of her touch, normally a comfort, couldn't stop my fear. And my fears grew when I realized she was crying too.

Life took on a new sort of chaos then. Dad worked constantly. Mom moved to the big city with Jonathan, where he could receive the treatment he needed. Grandparents moved nearby to care for the healthy kids, my other brother and myself. Relatives in the big city hosted us often, which gave the kids a chance to see Mom and Jonathan. The healthy brother was selected as a donor for Jonathan's bone marrow transplant. A surprise pregnancy added a new sibling to the family, a baby sister whom Jonathan adored.

Then, after over a year's battle, Jonathan relapsed. A spinal tap revealed cancer cells in the spinal fluid. There was nothing else the doctors could do.

That last week, family and friends from all over the country traveled to see him one last time. For the first time any of us could remember, he was too lethargic to cause trouble. His sleepy eyes seemed out of focus, and he reached his little hand towards something none of us this side of heaven could see.

And then, just as the summer began, he was gone.

From then on, the chaos was inside of me. Day after day, the grief I carried grew heavier and heavier. I wrestled with questions too immense for a nine-year-old to handle. Why did my brother have to die? What was the point of life if it would just end anyway? Wouldn't it be better to end it all sooner rather than later? After all, life is full of pain; death seemed the only escape.

I considered how I would do it—how I would end my own life. Firearms were stashed away, far out of my reach. Overdosing wasn't an option either; my parents didn't give the kids access to the medicine cabinet. The only tools easily accessible were kitchen knives, which sat out on the counter. I handled at least one every time I loaded or unloaded the dishwasher. And every time a knife found its way into my hand, demon depression would hiss, *Now!*

But every time I thought I could do it, my resolve crumbled. Would it hurt? Would it really be worth it? It would be such a *big* sin. Would God forgive me if I went through it with? If it was the last thing I ever did?

Finally, after weeks of back and forth, desperation drove me to the first place I should have gone: the arms of my Heavenly Father.

I threw myself across my bed and wept. "Take me home, Lord," I begged Him. "Let my pain end. I don't want to live on this earth any longer; I want to see my brother again!" But as I cried out, something changed.

The turmoil ebbed away, leaving stillness in its wake. Suddenly, there was peace beyond my understanding, a gentle reassurance, and a comforting hand. A deep impression was laid on my heart, not in audible words, but in a still small Voice: *It's not your time yet. I still have a plan and a purpose for you.*

As the sobs subsided, chagrin swept through me. What a foolish and selfish request I had made, asking the God who created the universe to kill me where I lay. What would my mother do if she lost another child? My father? My living brother and my new baby sister?

I wiped my tears and stood. That gentle reassurance filled me with new strength, and the weight I'd carried since my brother's diagnosis was no longer a crushing burden.

I'd always thought peace was a lack of chaos or pain. The thought of experiencing peace in the midst of pain—the kind of peace Paul experienced in his prison cell—was far more than I could comprehend. Perhaps the problem was that I had let the world determine my definition of "peace" rather than looking at how God defines it.

The clearest picture of God's peace can be found in the Hebrew word for peace: *shalom*. Ancient Hebrew letters carried symbolic meanings along with sounds. In some words, these symbols can paint a picture of what the word truly means.

For example, the word *shalom* can be broken down into three root letters: *shin*, *lamed*, and *mem*. The first letter, *shin*, is a picture of an open hand. It symbolizes hunger or demand and means "to consume" or "to destroy." The last letter, *mem*, is a picture of waves on the water. It is a picture of rough seas, symbolizing water and chaos.

It doesn't make sense, does it? How can a word describing "peace" contain pictures of chaos and destruction?

The answer is found in middle letter, the symbol at the heart of the word: *lamed.* It is a picture of a shepherd's staff, a symbol of protection and care.

This changes the entire meaning. *Shalom* isn't just a picture of chaos and destruction—it's a picture of a Shepherd leading His sheep safely in the middle of the chaos and destruction. *Shalom*, biblical peace, is trusting in and following God even when we don't feel particularly peaceful, because we know that the One who calmed the wind and the waves will see us safely through our own personal storms.

More than a decade after Jonathan's death, I still miss him. I struggle with depression. I still wrestle with anxiety. Every now and then, a sinister voice will whisper words of harm and self-destruction. But now I know with full confidence: I need not be anxious for *anything*, nor should I let my heart be troubled. For as long as Jonathan was breathing—and even now that he is gone—God had a plan and a purpose for him. And for as long as I am breathing, God still has a plan and a purpose for me.

And even in the middle of the chaos and the destruction in the world around me, I know I can trust in the Good Shepherd to guide me safely through the storm. He's never left me nor forsaken me, even during the most painful and chaotic moments in my life.

Now, like my mother before me, I can laugh when troubles come, because I know that He is with me. I don't have to fear the future, because the Good Shepherd guards me; His rod and His staff comfort me.

And the chaos continues.

"GROWING IN THE LORD"
Caridad Rivera

When we talk about prayer, we talk about an ever growing aspect of our spiritual life. We may start with the very basics, but as we continue on, our prayer life grows. When I first came to the Lord, I only used to say:

Our Father who art in heaven ...(**Matthew 9-15; Luke 11:2-4 KJV**). It was a simple prayer because at the time that was all I knew, but then I began to add to my prayer list family, friends, brothers in Christ etc., and before I knew it, the list got longer and longer.

For a beginner, like me, at the time it was easier to make a schedule and write down my prayer list. There were times when on my prayer, while praying for one person, the name of another person would come to my mind. So, I would make a parenthesis and pray for that name that just came to mind as well.

Many times, the Holy Spirit will guide you in prayer. Sometimes we will find ourselves praying for things that we don't know or intend to pray about. When that happens, it is because at the moment the Holy Spirit is guiding us on what to pray about.

One day when I was asleep, in the early hours of the morning, I heard a voice wake me up and tell me to pray, and I said I know I have to pray at the time I usually pray, but the voice said pray now.

I answered and said its 3:00 AM in the morning. I'm tired and I want to go to back to sleep. I was kind of new at prayer and didn't know how to discern what had just happened, but I thought to myself the enemy is not going to tell me to pray, so this must be the Lord.

So, as I began my prayer, the name of a sister from church came to my mind. I heard clearly there's an argument that has lifted up in the house of the sister between her and the husband, and you need to intercede in prayer now.

So, I began to pray, rebuke strongholds, and came against anything that was bringing up arguments in the household.

The next day I shared with the sister while in church that last night the Lord told me to pray for her. She opened her eyes wide and said at what time? I told her around 3:00A.M.

She informed me that she had gotten into an argument with her husband that doesn't serve the Lord and it got very ugly, and had escalated to the point that he wanted to hit her, and that she feared for her life. I was like Lord, I couldn't have known something like that and only did because of you woke me up to pray.

At first, I thought I was dreaming, but since I wanted to know for sure, I dared to ask the sister. She said this was God because no one else knows about what happened last night. Two things God did confirm to me is that He is aware of my situation and touched someone to intercede in prayer at that time and also at the same time, He can use you for an experience with the Lord. So, now you have no more doubts it was the Lord. Like my dearly beloved brothers in Christ, there will be many times when the Lord interrupts our scheduled prayer times, don't be surprised or doubt because one thing I know is that the devil will never tell you to pray for someone. He is in the business of destroying families, not uniting them.

Read the following verses:

(1 John 5:14-15,) And this is the confidence that we have in him, that, if we ask anything according to his will, he heareth us: And if we know that he hears us, whatsoever we ask, we know that we have the petitions that we desired of him; (Matthew 6:7-8), But when ye pray, use not vain repetitions, as the heathen do: for they think that they shall be heard for their much speaking. Be not ye therefore like unto them: for your Father knoweth what things ye have need of, before ye ask him. (Luke 12:30)

(Ephesians 2:18), For through him we both have access by one Spirit unto the Father.

Another thing that happens as your prayer and spiritual life grows, is that your faith will also grow, and you will have personal experiences with the Lord. The Lord begins to show you areas in your life that need to change. We come from the world with all kinds of bad habits, some visible, others hidden inside. But when you give your life to the Lord, He starts to work in you. He starts to cleanse you through His Word.

(Philippians 1:6,) Being confident of the very thing, that he which have begun a good work in you will perform it until the day of Jesus Christ.

That brings me to another important part of the Christian life and that is reading the Word of God. When I was lost, I never had any feelings whatsoever to read the Word of God. I had heard of it, but to me it was like an old book. The mentality I had was completely erroneous, as you can see. When I started reading the Bible, I could not understand it. I read in English and in Spanish and still could not understand it. I was frustrated because I knew how to read in both languages very well, but for some reason I could not understand the Word of God. I would go to Sunday school to hear the lesson, but it would not stay with me. I felt like it was a waste of time because I couldn't get it. I was so embarrassed that I didn't want anyone to know, much less, have anyone ask me any questions about the Word of God because I couldn't answer at all. I hungered for the presence of the Lord and wanted to understand the Word of God. I decided to include in my daily prayer for this.

One day a preacher came to our church to preach about the book of Revelation. I was completely confused and secretly decided I was not going to continue to go to Sunday school since I couldn't understand, so I was just going to attend the services and that was it. I went home to cry, my husband asked me, what happened? I said I can't understand the Word of God. How is it possible that I can read perfectly fine in two languages, yet when it comes to reading and understanding the Word of God I can't get it. In my frustration, I told him that is it ... I give up! I will just go to church and be a statue; I will not respond to any question if they ask me because I don't want to look dumb. To my surprise, the co-pastor was a very good friend of my husband for many years and he came to visit with his wife and family. So, I asked him why it is I can't understand the Word of God, by the way I'm confused with the preaching of Revelation. After a while after he left, but before they left, they said a prayer. I went to sleep ... BUT, the Lord had other plans with me.

I had the most amazing dream; it was simple enough for me to understand. I was digging in the dirt like I was digging for a treasure or for something valuable. I didn't know why, but in the dream, I was digging. When I hit something, I stopped digging and carefully brushed the dirt on top of the box I was holding, then I heard a voice that told me to open it up and start reading the gospels first. So, through this dream I understood the Lord wanted me to start reading the gospels first. The may not be a big idea for some people, but for me it was a beautiful blessing. The idea of not going to Sunday school completely left and I concentrated on reading the Bible.

(Romans 8:5-8), For they that are after the flesh do mind the things of the flesh; but they that are after the Spirit, the things of the Spirit. For to be carnally minded is death; but to be spiritually minded is life and peace. Because the carnal mind is enmity against God: for it is not subject to the law of God, neither indeed can be. So, then they that are in the flesh cannot please God. But ye are not in the flesh, but in the Spirit, if so be that the Spirit of God dwell in you. No if any man have not the Spirit of Christ, he is none of his. And if Christ be in you, the body is dead because of sin; But

the Spirit of him that raised up Jesus from the dead dwell in you, he that raised up Christ from the dead shall also quicken your mortal bodies by his Spirit that dwelleth in you.

Therefore, bretheren, we are debtors, not to the flesh, to live after the flesh. For if ye live after the flesh, ye shall die; but if ye live through the Spirit and do mortify the deeds of the body, ye shall live. For as many as are led by the Spirit of God, they are the sons of God).

Read also *(Ephesians 4:17), This I say therefore, and testify in the Lord, that ye walk not as other Gentiles walk, in the vanity of their mind; ...*

(Proverbs 15:26), The thoughts of the wicked are an abomination to the Lord: but the words of the pure are pleasant words; (Psalm 92:6), A brutish man knoweth not; neither doth a fool understand this;

(Galatians 5:16; 25), If we live in the Spirit, let us also walk in the spirit. This I say then, walk in the spirit, and ye shall not fulfill the lust of the flesh; (Ephesians 4:23), And be renewed in the spirit of your mind; (2 Corinthians 10:3), For though we walk in the flesh, we do not war after the flesh; (1 John 1:7), But if we walk in the light, as he is in the light, we have fellowship one with another, and the blood of Jesus Christ his Son cleanseth us from all sin.

I understood that when you have a carnal mind, you can't understand the things of the Lord. I was trying my best to understand the Word of God, but I still had a carnal mind. The Lord still needed to work in me. It is so easy to pick up bad habits, but so difficult to pick up good habits.

After this I had another dream, this one was completely different. I was on a very high mountain, I don't know how I got there, but there all I know is that I wasn't alone, someone else was here with me. I heard the voice tell me you see that little bottle it has a drop of oil, open it and let the drop of oil touch the tip of your tongue. The Lord is going to transform you inside out. And so, I did as soon as the oil touched my tongue, I started to feel something happening inside of me. It was like that little bit of oil went all the way down inside of me and started to break chains, my way of talking, etc. I felt like I was a new person. I was excited and happy when I woke up.

Prayer is indispensable for the believer; it's important to read and have knowledge of the Word of God but it is also important to keep a prayerful life. The Holy Spirit can guide you, even bring the Word of God to memory when you are facing difficult times. There are certain things that you cannot know unless the Holy Spirit reveals them to you.

That brings me to another experience; this one was a brother from church. I didn't know what was going on. All I know was that I was reading the Bible, and the Lord directed me to pray for the brother, and the only thing he informed me was that the brother had been accused of something, but he is innocent. And so, that's exactly what I did; I just prayed for the brother, included him in my daily prayer without even telling him anything.

One day I saw his wife and she looked very sad, so I called her and told her I don't know what is going on but the other day the Lord directed me to pray for your household and the only thing the Lord informed me was that he was innocent and was falsely accused of something. She cried and cried, I told whatever he is being accused of, the charges will be dropped because he is innocent; you just wait and see. I kept the conversation to myself and didn't tell anyone. The Lord showed me that there are certain things we can say, and some things are for us just to pray.

One day, the wife testifies about the problem and she stated the charges against her husband were all dropped, and he was found innocent. I was like, *"Wow, the enemy tried to destroy this family, the wife was worried and even doubting her husband, but the Lord stepped in to save this marriage."* When you lead a life of prayer, the Holy Spirit will guide you, sometimes you don't know or understand why you are going through hardship in life, but you have to be patient and trust the Lord, even if you don't understand or are falsely be accused of something. Leave it in God's hands, He knows what to do.

No matter what giant you may be facing, be not discouraged because God will show you that you are not alone. You just trust in the Lord and see how He works things out for you. No problem is too big for Him to handle. Surely if He created the heavens, the Earth and all living things, He can handle whatever impossibilities lay ahead.

(Joshua 1:8-9), This book of the law shall not depart out of thy mouth; but thou shall mediate therein day and night, that thou mayest observe to do according to all that is written therein; for then thou shall make thy way prosperous, and then thou shall have good success. Have I not commanded thee? Be strong and of a good courage; be not afraid, neither be thou dismayed: for the Lord they God is with thee whithersoever thou goest).

Hebrews 11 talks about great men of faith that faced adversities and even when things seemed impossible, God stepped in to demonstrate that He is an Awesome God and that there is nothing impossible for Him. So, if you are feeling down or going through something today, trust in the Lord. Prayer makes our faith stronger, and just like the commercial "milk does a body good" well, prayer is great for our spiritual body. Make it a habit to take out time for prayer, reading the Word of God, meditate on the Word of God, fast when possible and do vigils on your own if possible for spiritual growth. You will be amazed at how the Lord works in you and through you. Finally, I leave the following verses with you.

(1 Thessalonians 5:17), Pray without ceasing; (John 15:7), If ye abide in me, and my words abide in you, ye shall ask what ye will, and it shall be done unto you; (Romans 5:26), Likewise the Spirit also helpeth our infirmities: for we know not we should pray for as we ought but the Spirit itself maketh intercession for us with groanings which cannot be uttered; (1 Timothy 2:8), I will therefore that men pray everywhere, lifting up holy hands, without doubting; (Matthew 21:22), And all things, whatsoever ye shall ask in prayer, believing, ye shall receive; (Acts 6:4), But we will give ourselves to prayer, and to the ministry of the word.

As the years have gone by I have never regretted giving my life to Christ; it was the best decision I ever made in my life, and I am forever thankful to God for the opportunity of serving Him. May the Lord continue to bless you and in your walk with Christ and most of all... hold to the Lord for the rest of your life.

God bless, your Sister in Christ C. Rivera

ONE DROP OF GOD'S FAVOR
By: Just one of His kids

I'm always amazed out how God's favor can change things for the good, as quickly as something bad manifests. I have this saying being "one drop of God's favor can change everything."

I came to this not merely as a cool saying, but rather something that I have seen over and over again in my life and the lives of others. It is a word of encouragement that I use many times when ministering to others, saying "one drop of God's favor can change everything" followed by "and God is much bigger than your problem or situation is."

We recently encountered a situation where our car broke down and the cost to repair the vehicle was well over $2,000.00. To top it off, this all happened the very week that our daughter started her new school year. For those of you that are a one car family, you know how challenging being a one car family can be at times.

We soon found ourselves with no transportation and paying $25.00 a day to a ride service to get our daughter to school. This meant that each morning mom ,and our daughter, had to wait for the ride service and once the ride service came they both would then take off for school and then the ride service would have to drop mom back off at home again. Then the whole process started over again when it was time for our daughter to be picked up and brought home. The daily stress of hoping that the ride service would show up on time to get our daughter to school and also to pick her up from school each day was in itself, very stressful.

The day that the car broke down, the vehicle was towed to a local repair shop and the towing bill was $197.00. Unfortunately, the particular repair shop that the emergency services had the car towed to determined that they couldn't make the type of repairs that were required. This left us with no other option but to have the car towed either to another repair station or back home to further determine the best way to go forward.

Where God's favor first started manifesting was when we had the car towed from the repair shop back home. The first tow which consisted of towing the car one mile from where it broke down at to the repair station ran $197.00; however, the second tow having the car towed from the repair station to our home which is over three miles was only $70.00. Huge difference.

Considering that many years ago back in the day I spent years working in the automotive field, I wanted an opportunity to look the car over, do some leg work with regards to repairs and cost and to make calls to various local repair shops to find the right repair shop to have the car fixed at.

After about a week of using the ride services at $25.00 per day and using a local grocery delivery services which by the way is actually a great way to do your grocery shopping without all the hassles of driving to the grocery store, dealing with those that shop from the center of the isle rather than moving to the right or left, so people can get by and then dealing with long lines at the check-out. Using an online grocery store delivery service where you order online and they deliver the groceries to your door is a blessing in itself.

The next thing that happened, which is nothing less than God's favor, is my wife was sharing with a friend that our car had broke down. It was simply a conversation that came about as her friend asked how she was. As the conversation continued forth about other things in general, my wife was then talking with the woman's husband. As the conversation was taking place, her friend handed her a folded check and said this is for you, know that you are loved. My wife was somewhat taken by this and said thank you and simply placed the folded check in her purse without even looking at it. The conversation then soon ended as other people had walked up.

About an hour later my wife comes to me and says, "You will never believe what just happened and explained the above to me." I said that was very nice of her. It was at this point that my wife said, "The check is for enough to cover the cars repair bill." I must admit that at that point I became somewhat silent knowing that God was in the boat with us.

Next, we had our car towed to the dealership to be repaired. Even though taking one's car to the dealership is much more expensive than a local repair shop, we were getting nothing more than confusion with regards to costs, what needed to be done and what didn't need to be done from various repair shops. Plus, this particular dealership said they would provide us with a loaner car while they evaluated what needed to be repaired and the cost. This was another place where God's favor came into play because in our neck of the woods it is rare for a repair shop to even give you a ride home after dropping your car off for repairs, let alone provide you with a free loaner car.

So, after my wife signed all the paperwork to get the car evaluated for repairs came the loaner car, of course, we were simply hoping for something with 4 wheels that ran decent, was safe to drive and looked ok.

The next think I know, my wife comes home with a brand new car with new car plates, and I'm thinking what is this?

The loaner car that she was provided with was a brand new 2018 top of the line SUV. In examining the car, it had less than 500 miles on it. It was brand new, the floor mats were still wrapped in plastic. I was in shock and for my wife, she grinned from ear-to-ear. Days later, I would look in the glove box and find the new car sticker. It was a $48,000.00 new car loaner car.

You see what started out to be a very bad situation is turning out to actually be a blessing. Sure, our car broke down and we did encounter some financial losses, stress and aggravation. However, God made a way where there seemed to be no way by providing us with the money needed to repair the vehicle, discounted towing prices, a beautiful car to drive while our car is being repaired and in the midst of what started out as a very bad situation, God's favor is bringing us through it all and into a place of Victory.

Remember, one drop of God's favor can change things and God is much bigger than your problems.

A Servants Heart

Some years back, I had the humble privilege to serve in a homeless outreach at a local church. Through such, I have seen love and compassion bring change in the lives of others over and over again and in the simplest of ways.

One perfect example of this was a woman that came to the outreach for some food. In a voice of shame with her head down, she said, "Could I possibly have some bread?" You see, here was a homeless woman in probably her late 50's and in her situation, that is all that she felt that she was worth. A loaf of bread.

I recall the look on her face, the sorrow and the sadness in her eyes, the fear that was gripping her as she asked for a loaf of bread as the fear of rejection played a part in this. Over the years, I would encounter hundreds of people like this.

I then immediately grabbed a large box as she looked at me with tears in her eyes, overwhelmed with her lips quivering and somewhat speechless and said, "Sure, you can have all the food that you want." She then said, in complete shock, "Really, I can have some food?"

You see within this woman's situation, her self-worth had hit rock bottom. Yet, in that one moment as I simply extended mercy and compassion to her, things changed. Encouragement and hope sprang forth and through such, hopelessness was being defeated.

The same woman that came with expressions of being worthless, fearful of rejection, overwhelmed with shame and sorrow, she would eventually leave with a sense of joy, feeling loved, as if someone cared and with a big smile on her face.

God worked through that situation and I had the opportunity to pray with her, minister to her and simply spend time with her.

Another example at the same food outreach was a man, his wife and their little boy who came in wanting to get some food. All three of them looked stressed out. I recall that the wife was quite upset about their situation, the father was clothed with shame and the little boy looked deeply depressed and sad. There is nothing worse than seeing depression and sadness in a child's eyes.

Over to the right of me was a large container with some goods that had been donated to the church. On the very top of the box was a really nice skateboard.

So, I leaned over towards the father and said, "Does your son have a skateboard?" and the father somewhat taken by the questions said, "No, he doesn't." So, I asked, "Can I give him one?" and the father said, "Sure."

I then kneeled down to this little boy of about 8 and said, "Do you have a skateboard?" and he said in a very sad voice "No, I don't, we don't even have a home." So, I said,

"Would you like to have a skateboard?" and he said "Yes, as his voice sparked up."

I then reached over and grabbed the skateboard and handed it to him. Immediately his sadness left him, and his face lit up with joy and excitement, as he examined the skateboard. As for the father and mother, they both started tearing up as they saw the expressions of sadness on their son's face turn into expressions of joy.

You see in the midst of all that family was encountering at the time, the simplicity of giving a skateboard to a little boy made a huge difference in his life and in theirs.

After spending time with the little boy and ministering to his father and mother, I got the humble privilege to pray for the family and help them get some much needed food. I must admit I walked away with tears in my eyes wishing that I could have done more. But in that one moment of time, I was able to be used of God in the simplest of ways.

As the years would pass, I would met hundreds of people through this out reach. Single men and women, single mothers, families, homeless people and people that were encountering difficult times.

Regardless of the situation or circumstances that they were encountering. The simplicity of treating them with dignity, encouraging them and assisting them in their needs made a huge difference. Just the fact that someone cared brought joy to their heart and gave them hope.

Remember, we can all make a difference in the simplest of ways and sometimes it's the little things that count.

PRINCESS WARRIOR

Luke 3:22 says; "And the Holy Spirit descended on him in bodily form, like a dove; and a voice came from heaven, 'You are my beloved Son;[a] with you I am well pleased.' "

Have you ever looked back on your life journey and asked where was God? I have spent the past five years or so looking at my life story and asking God to show me where He was as evil tried to steal my soul. John 10:10 states; "The thief comes only to steal and kill and destroy. I came that they may have life and have it abundantly." I received Jesus as my Lord and Savior at the age of eight. The day of my salvation was the day I was sealed with the Holy Spirit. Ephesians 1:13 says; "In him you also, when you heard the word of truth, the gospel of your salvation, and believed in him, were sealed with the promised Holy Spirit."

As I have asked God to reveal to me where He was during the difficult and challenging times of my life He has given me the following image:

As I walk down a windy dirt path my mind is resting on the beauty of the green trees and foliage surrounding me. Occasionally I see patches of wild flowers scattered along the path. The sun, shining through the trees, provides a warmth that reaches to the depth of my soul. My body and soul are at peace. As I continue to walk I notice the trees are getting more and more dense and the light is getting brighter. I get to the end of the path and I cannot go any further. One more step and I will fall down a cliff. As I stand at the top of the cliff looking down into the valley below I become curious about what I am seeing.

The valley is surrounded by what I would describe as storm clouds. They are not black but certainly grey skies and no sun can penetrate the clouds. There is also some green pastures and a body of still water. It reminds me of the description in Psalms 23 where David talks about God leading beside clear and still water and though I walk through the valley of the shadow of death I will feel no evil for thou (God) art with me.

As I continue to watch from afar I see images standing by the clear water. One is the image of Jesus who clearly holds an infant in His arms. Beside Him is a toddler who finds comfort in playing around the hem of Jesus but not wandering off. Another figure that appears to be an eight- year-old little girl sitting by the water with what appears to be armor surrounding her. Her white gown is ripped and stained with dried blood, her face has tear stains that have run down her cheeks. Her face is partially hidden by the helmet of salvation that covers her soft brown hair. The rest of the armor of God surrounds her due to an uncertainty as to what she should do with all those pieces. Some of them weighing more than she does. Ephesians 1:14-16 says that we should put on the armor of God. The armor according this passage is "Stand therefore, having fastened on the belt of truth, and having put on the breastplate of righteousness, and, as shoes for your feet, having put on the readiness given by the gospel of peace. In all circumstances take up the shield of faith, with which you can extinguish all the flaming darts of the evil one; and take the helmet of salvation, and the sword of the Spirit, which is the word of God..." For an eight-year-old that is rather confusing. The helmet is her salvation which she got at the day of repentance and the day she was sealed by the Holy Spirit.

Standing off to the side is an adolescent female, approximately fourteen or fifteen years of age. She is very quiet but also very angry. She is confused because she carries most of the pain and responsibility of being abused physically, sexually, spiritually and emotionally for the past several years of her life by a pastor.

My attention is suddenly drawn away from the figures on the embankment to the still waters. There appears to be some stirring in the water. As I look closer I am in awe as there appears to be a person emerging from the water. This figure appears to be that of a princess. A princess that is clothed in the full armor of God. This is a woman who is confident and faithful and is armed for battle, yet you can also see the scars and pain she has endured during her life's journey. The scars add to the beauty that radiates from deep within the depths of this princess. As she fully emerges, she absorbs the figures of Jesus and the young parts that were standing on the side of the water. She encompass' all these parts and clothed in the grace and love of Jesus she takes on the form of a princess warrior. She is ready to step into the battle for which God has called her. Her sword is engraved with the words: *"She grew in stature and wisdom."*

This image is a work in progress. I think so often we go around saying we want to know what God's will for us is or question where He was or is in the difficult times, but we don't stop and take the time to listen for His answer. I know I am guilty of that most of the time. I am learning however, that when I stop and become more prayerful and ask God to reveal Himself to me through the Scripture He always is faithful and shows up. It isn't that God is not present but that more often than not we miss Him because we do not take the time to seek Him. I am seeing where God was an everlasting presence in my times of trauma. Satan could not steal me from Him because I had been sealed with the presence and protection of the Holy Spirit.

I encourage you to stop and ask God to reveal to you something you are wanting to know or that you are struggling with. Over the next couple weeks. All it takes is a simple prayer. My prayer in this season of my life has been as simple as, "God reveal to me through this scripture of the Bible study where you were when I was being abused?" That was all it took for me to see God in my pain. He was holding and protecting me as He molded me into His daughter. A daughter with whom He is well pleased. Give it a try - you won't be disappointed.

.

Made in the USA
Monee, IL
06 November 2019